A Critical Introduction to the Study of Religion

A Critical Introduction to the Study of Religion

Craig Martin

Routledge
Taylor & Francis Group
LONDON AND NEW YORK

First published 2012 by Equinox Publishing Ltd, an imprint of Acumen

Published 2014 by Routledge
2 Park Square, Milton Park, Abingdon, Oxon OX14 4RN
711 Third Avenue, New York, NY 10017, USA

Routledge is an imprint of the Taylor and Francis Group, an informa business

ISBN: 978-1-84553-991-7 (hardback)
ISBN: 978-1-84553-992-4 (paperback)

British Library Cataloguing-in-Publication Data
A catalogue record for this book is available from the British Library.

Typeset by JS Typesetting Ltd, Porthcawl, Mid Glamorgan.

I ask the pardon of those teachers who, in dreadful conditions, attempt to turn the few weapons they can find in the history and learning they "teach" against the ideology, the system and the practices in which they are trapped. They are a kind of hero. But they are rare and how many (the majority) do not even begin to suspect the "work" the system (which is bigger than they are and crushes them) forces them to do.

Louis Althusser, *Lenin and Philosophy and Other Essays* (2001, 106)

This book is dedicated to such heroes, including Erica

Contents

Acknowledgments

This book has benefitted greatly from the overwhelming generosity of peers and colleagues who were willing to field ideas, read drafts of chapters, or read the entire manuscript.

From St Thomas Aquinas College, I first want to thank my undergraduate students who suffered through the early drafts. Particular mention goes to Emily Hough, Angela Banta, and Dillon Challener for encouraging me to foreground the practical and political consequences of classification in Chapter 2. In addition, for Chapter 6 Valissa Hicks created the visual depiction of the circular relationship of authority and projection; Katie Roepken created the inkblot. Thanks go to Professors C.J. Churchill and Neerja Chaturvedi for organizing the faculty research retreats at which I tried out some of the material in Chapter 3 and received useful feedback. Thanks also go to the participants in the humanities division theory reading group, especially Robert Murray, Barbara Yontz, Nicole de Fee, and Neerja Chaturvedi; the conversations we had on the subject of authenticity helped me work out some of the ideas in Chapter 7. Robert Trawick, my office mate and fellow religion professor, deserves thanks for all of the office conversations and pedagogical commiseration. I want to thank Ellen Chayet for continually encouraging me to foreground questions regarding domination and oppression in the classroom. Last, thanks go to Nicole de Fee and Ryan Wynne for general moral support—they kept me from going crazy as I attempted to balance my research with my teaching.

As I work at a college with only one other faculty member in religious studies, I often depend upon Facebook for intellectual engagement on theoretical and methodological questions related to the study of religion. I want to thank my Facebook friends in general, many of whom engaged me in numerous online conversations while I was working on this book; special mention goes to Russell McCutcheon, Nathan Rein, Tim Murphy, Tim Morgan, Kenny Paul Smith, Bill Arnal, Aldea Mulhern, Chris Zeichmann, Nicholas Dion, and Robert Trawick.

I was fortunate to have many friends willing to read part of the manuscript, including Terry Rey, Marcel Parent, Luke Roelofs, Tim Murphy, and Stephen Benko. Special thanks go to my friends Donovan Schaefer and Jeremy Vecchi, who all but co-wrote Chapter 7; their assistance with that chapter was invaluable. Colleagues who generously read and commented on a manuscript draft in its entirety include Aaron Hughes, Bill Arnal, Jim West, Chris Zeichmann, and Shawn Loner. The number of volunteers willing to read and comment on this book astonished me, and I am greatly in their debt.

As always, I want to note that the views expressed in this book are not necessarily the views of those who helped me improve it.

Thanks go to Tak Toyoshima, creator and illustrator of *Secret Asian Man* comics, who permitted me to reproduce the comic strip in Chapter 1. Some of the material in Chapter 1 previously appeared in "Delimiting religion," *Method and Theory in the Study of Religion* 21/2 (2009). Some of the material in Chapter 6 previously appeared in "How to read an interpretation: Interpretive strategies and the maintenance of authority," *Bible and Critical Theory* 5/1 (2009). Thanks go to the editors for permitting me to use that material here.

Credits for figures within the book are given below the figure caption; those figures without a credit line are either created by me or in the public domain. Figures 2.2–2.4 and 4.1–4.3 are copyrighted using a Creative Commons Copyright 2.0; in each case the individual who owns the copyright has designated the images as available for commercial use with attribution. I have identified the Flickr.com username of the individual who owns the copyright for each in the credit line.

Last, thanks go to Erica, to whom this book is dedicated—you are one of my heroes.

Preface

Societies, human relations, social artifacts, etc. do not simply exist; they are created by human languages, practices, habits, and so on. However, most of us take the world as it is presented to us for granted: we rarely stop to question how it got to be the way it did, or what social and historical conditions made our particular world possible. When we take the world for granted in this way, it becomes almost "natural" to us, and as such we cannot see the social work that produced it. This process by which social things are taken for granted as natural is called "naturalization" or "mystification." The task of critical theory is to demystify the world: to look at the social conditions that make the apparently natural world possible. In addition, critical theorists reflect on how those conditions and the world they create serve the interests of some groups at the expense of others.

Perhaps the clearest example of mystification can be found in grocery store checkout lanes: most of us have seen pictures of extremely thin models—with literally unreal proportions—on the cover of magazines like *Cosmopolitan* or *Vanity Fair*. However, most of us also know by now that these photos have gone through an editing process, using Photoshop or a similar image editing program. In fact, we can access videos on YouTube showing precisely the sort of editing process such photos go through. The videos show how acne and wrinkles are removed, breasts are enlarged, waists are shrunk, and so on. Those videos are *demystifying* the photos on the magazine covers: they show that there is nothing "natural" about the way women look on the cover of *Cosmopolitan*, and go on to show what processes took place to make the final cover photo possible. Feminist critical theorists take the process of demystification a step further by asking questions such as the following: What social conditions allowed this idealized image of femininity to come into existence? How is this idealization similar to or different from the way women were idealized in the past? Does this idealization serve the interests of women?

An example more germane to our topic might be the following. Most Muslims might look at the Qur'an and think: "sacred book." A critical theorist, by contrast, will look at it and attempt to demystify its assumed "sacredness" by asking these sorts of questions: How and when was this book written? Who wrote it? What might its author (or authors) have wanted to accomplish? What social circumstances were in place that led a group of people to see this book as holy or as more authoritative than other books? Why do some people view this book as authoritative, but not others? What social consequences follow from that? Whose interests are served when this book is taken for granted as sacred? (The same critical questions could also be asked of the Torah, the Bible, the Lotus Sutra, or any other "sacred book.")

It should be clear that the word "critical" in "critical theory" is different from the colloquial sense: the purpose of critical theory is not to show what is wrong with an object of analysis, to attack it or "tear it down." Rather, the purpose of critical theory is to demystify what we take for granted. Of course, sometimes the practice of demystification is *unflattering*—some Muslims might be uncomfortable with the idea that the "sacredness" of the Qur'an is in part a product of historical or social forces—but saying unflattering things is not the primary goal of critical theory. This book is "critical" in the sense that I hope to demystify society and religion; this book focuses on what conditions make society possible, how religious traditions contribute to its creation and contestation, and whose interests are served by particular formations of religion and society.

This book therefore introduces readers to a theory of how the elements of cultural traditions can be used in the creation, maintenance, and contestation of social order. It is designed to be a text suitable for an undergraduate course, and could be used to anchor an introductory course—whether a so-called "world religions" course or an introductory "theory and method" type of course. In either case it would, of course, require supplementary material. I currently use this text in my introductory course in the following manner: I typically have the students read a chapter, read a primary text or other data, and then ask them to analyze the data using the critical vocabulary in the chapter. For example, my students read the chapter on legitimation (Chapter 5) and watch M. Night Shyamalan's *The Village* (2004), after which we analyze the cultural tools used by the community in the film and consider what legitimating social functions they serve, as well as how the social functions are more important than their purported "meaning." We follow it up by reading selections from the Bhagavad Gita and considering how the story could have been used to reflect and reinforce class hierarchy in ancient India.

This book could also be used in a more advanced undergraduate theory and method course in which students are introduced to anthropology of religion, psychology of religion, philosophy of religion, and so on—this text could stand in for critical theory of religion or sociofunctional approaches in general.

What follows is not original; rather, it draws on the theories of Karl Marx, Émile Durkheim, Max Weber, Antonio Gramsci, Mary Douglas, Peter Berger, Thomas Luckmann, Louis Althusser, Raymond Williams, Michel Foucault, Anthony Giddens, David Kertzer, Pierre Bourdieu, Marshall Sahlins, Bruce Lincoln, and Russell McCutcheon. This project started, in fact, as a rewrite of the first two chapters of Berger's *The Sacred Canopy* for some students who (understandably) found Berger's vocabulary and diction impenetrable. Almost everything below follows from the spirit of Marx, Durkheim, and Weber, whose theories Berger was attempting to synthesize in *The Sacred Canopy*. In any case, my hope is to make these theorists' ways of seeing how societies and religion work accessible to students or general readers.

I want to emphasize the fact that this book is not designed to introduce students to specific theorists of religion or offer a history of important theories, but rather to give students the skills to analyze cultural traditions from a sociological, critical theory, or cultural studies perspective. Although the works of Marx, Durkheim, and Weber lie behind the material presented, the reader will not find a biography of each thinker or a section introducing the main ideas of each. As an instructor, I am much more interested in having introductory students—who may only take one religion class in their academic careers—be able to understand and use, for instance, Pierre Bourdieu's concept of habitus than to know something about Bourdieu's biography, his basic works, or who he borrowed the concept from.

Readers will notice that there are more examples from Christianity than from other religious traditions in this book. There are two reasons for that. First, my scholarly training has made me much more familiar with Christianity, so I feel more comfortable writing about that tradition than, say, Islam or Buddhism. Second, I teach at a school with a Catholic heritage; most of my students are at least nominally Catholic and have a prior familiarity with the basic cultural content of the Christian tradition. Consequently, Christian examples are the first I reach for in pedagogical contexts. I suspect that many readers will similarly have at least a minimal prior familiarity with Christianity. While I have included examples from a wide variety of other religious traditions, I introduce those examples without assuming any prior familiarity.

It is also worth noting that I unapologetically allow concerns about social domination to direct the choices I made when considering what to include in this book. I am in full agreement with Bruce Lincoln when he claims

> to view as immoral any discourse or practice that systematically operates to benefit the already privileged members of society at the expense of others, and I reserve the same judgment for any society that tolerates or encourages such discourses and practices. (Lincoln 1991b, 112)

These normative concerns are reflected in my primary teaching goals. They are, first, to demonstrate to students that societies are never set up in ways that serve everyone's interests equally, and, second, to give students the skills to identify who benefits and who does not, and how disproportionate social structures are legitimated and maintained. In this book I have therefore chosen to focus narrowly on how the elements of cultural traditions are utilized to create, reproduce, and contest social order—as well as how these relate to the interests of certain groups within that social order. Of course, this is only one aspect of religious traditions, but it is a rather important one, which is often either ignored or, when noticed, considered briefly or marginally. Hence I believe turning the spotlight in this direction is fully justified.

Chapter 1 considers the critical method used throughout the book. Chapters 2–4 offer a theory of society, and Chapters 5–7 offer a theory of religion. The last chapter is a case study: I provide a reading of Charles Sheldon's 1896 novel *In His Steps*, demonstrating how the method and theories proposed in this book shed light on a certain form of nineteenth-century Christianity. The matters covered in the chapters on society are assumed by the theory of religion proposed in the later chapters, particularly as I focus primarily on how culture contributes to the reproduction and contestation of social order. However, I have written each chapter so it can be read as a stand-alone essay, and the chapters can be read out of the order I've placed them in.

1

Studying Religion: Laying the Groundwork

What Is Religion?

This book purports to be about something called "religion," but what do we mean when we say "religion"? To what are we referring? Asking this question leads us into a number of difficult theoretical issues—some of which are considered in Chapter 2—but here we will attempt a simple answer.

The short answer to the question is that this book generally uses the word "religion" in the contemporary, colloquial, everyday sense. When we talk about "religions," we will refer to cultural traditions such as Christianity, Judaism, Buddhism, and so on.

In saying this, however, we are not offering a *definition* of religion—we are just pointing out how the word is typically used. This is the way we normally do things. If one is chatting with a two-year-old child still learning basic English vocabulary, and she wanted to know what a car was, one probably wouldn't offer a technical definition; one wouldn't say "a car is a human transportation device with four wheels and a combustion engine." Instead, one would probably just point: "See that? That's a car."

Why not offer some sort of official definition of religion? The problem is that we cannot formulate an official definition that fits with the everyday colloquial use of the word. Usually when we try to formulate a definition, we look at all the different things that word is applied to, and try to see what they have in common with each other. For instance, we could look at lions and tigers, and try to figure out what they each have in common with their own species that simultaneously distinguishes them from the other species: those big cats we call tigers all have stripes, and those big cats we call lions have manes (or at least the males in the species do). "Stripes" would go into our definition of tigers—since they all have that in common—and "manes" would go into our definition of lions. There would be more to it than this, but this would be a start.

However, this method of formulating a definition will not work when we come to all those things we commonly refer to as "religion," because *there are no features that are uniquely common to all the traditions we typically call religions.* People have tried to make an official definition that fits our colloquial everyday use, but they inevitably fail. Consider the following things one might find in the world, which the word religion might or might not group together:

Judaism	Indigenous cultures	Feng shui
Christianity	Practice of yoga	Visiting a medium
Islam	Personal meditation	Marxism or existentialism
Hinduism	Reading self-help books	The Metallica fan club
Buddhism	Reading astrology reports	American nationalism

Which of these things would be picked up by the word religion? I think most people would generally agree that the colloquial use of the term would probably group together all of the things in the first column (with a small question mark next to Buddhism for all of those people who say it is a philosophy and not a religion). From the second column, the term might include indigenous cultures or the practice of yoga (another couple of small question marks), but probably not the other things. Colloquial uses of the term religion rarely, if ever, include anything in the third column.

Now look at the following common definitions of religion; we can see that none of them will pick up the same thing that the colloquial use of the term picks up.

- *Religion as a "belief system."* This definition includes both more and less than the colloquial use. It will probably pick up Marxism or existentialism, for example. In addition, the Metallica fan club may well be organized around the belief that Metallica is the best band there ever was. However, some Jewish and Buddhist practitioners specifically emphasize that one's practice (ritual or meditative) is all that is important to them, and that one's beliefs are irrelevant for membership in their community. This definition would probably not pick up those particular forms of Judaism and Buddhism.

- *Religion as something that specifically concerns "supernatural" matters.* This definition will also group together more and less than the colloquial use. Insofar as some forms of Christianity and Buddhism are atheist, this sort of definition would not include those forms, although the colloquial use probably would. Also, this term might pick up astrology, feng shui, or visiting a medium, and some uses of ouija boards, although the colloquial use probably would not.
- *Religion as "matters of faith."* This sort of definition often trades on the association of "religion" with "faith" and the association of "science" with "reason." However, if we understand "faith" to be "faith in things that cannot be proven," then one will find "faith" in elements of *all* of the things on the list. It cannot be "proven" that Metallica is the best band ever, nor can the nationalist faith in America be "rationally" justified. At the same time, if we understand "reason" to concern "things that can be proven," then one will also find "reason" in elements of *all* of the things on the list. It seems "reasonable" to claim that a man named Gautama preached about *dukkha* a few centuries BCE, to claim that a man named Jesus lived, preached, and developed some sort of following in the first century, to claim that Metallica is a heavy metal rock band, or to claim that the 4th of July celebrates the day on which the Declaration of Independence was signed. These things are part of Buddhism, Christianity, the Metallica fan club, and American nationalism, but they are not simply matters of faith; they are facts. There are *both* matters of "faith" and matters of "reason" in every cultural tradition; the faith/reason binary will not neatly segregate those traditions colloquially called religions from other traditions.
- *Religion as concerning "the meaning of life."* I am very uncomfortable with this definition because concerns about the so-called "meaning of life" are rather recent and bourgeois. Ancient Jews and first-century Christians, for instance, didn't talk about the "meaning of life," and most poor people spend their lives searching more for the satisfaction of minimal needs than the "meaning of life." This vocabulary is really one of recent coinage, and is used most often by those who have the leisure time to search for

this sort of "meaning." This definition would not pick up much of anything prior to the twentieth century. However, we can take part of this idea, and transform it slightly; perhaps concerns about the "meaning of life" belong under the category of "concerns about one's place in a cosmology." This more general category will pick up all of the things the colloquial use of the term religion does, and several more. One can find concerns about one's place in a cosmology in some forms of yoga, self-help books, Marxism and existentialism, and some forms of American nationalism (those forms that focused on manifest destiny, for instance).

- *Religion as concerning "spirituality" or "spiritual well-being."* What this will pick up will depend on what one means by "spiritual," a vague term that is easily abused on account of its vagueness. Nevertheless, if we let "spiritual" be used broadly, this definition of religion will probably pick up all of the things the colloquial use does, as well as yoga, meditation, self-help books, and perhaps feng shui.
- *Religion as "communal institutions oriented around a set of beliefs, ritual practices, and ethical or social norms."* This definition—which is close to some scholarly uses of the word—will probably pick up all of the things the colloquial use does, but it will probably also pick up some forms of yoga (maybe not those forms that are simply exercise, but probably those that are communally practiced), Marxism, the Metallica fan club, and American nationalism. In fact, this definition is very broad, and would probably pick up a whole host of things not colloquially understood to be religious: karate centers, Oprah's book club, businesses that have an important corporate culture, the local university's department of religious studies, etc.

One might come a little closer to the colloquial use by combining the last definition with some qualification about the importance of supernatural elements. However, such a definition would still pick up American nationalism, which often has a theistic inflection, and would still fail to pick up atheist forms of some traditions colloquially called religions. *None of these definitions match the colloquial use exactly.*

The problem here is simple: the reason why we can't formulate a definition that fits the colloquial use is because *the colloquial use groups together dissimilar things.* All of those things we call "religions" simply do not share a set of core properties. A radical consequence of recognizing this fact is that we will not be able to make any *generalizations* about those cultural traditions we call religions. It is easy to make generalizations about something that has a precise definition: all "fish" live in water and breathe with gills. But a term like "sea creature" is broader than "fish," and groups together a wider variety of things, many of them dissimilar. We could say that "all fish breathe with gills," but we couldn't say "all sea creatures breathe with gills," because whales and dolphins do not. The word "religion" is much more like "sea creatures" than "fish"—a lot of different things are grouped together under the word religion—and that prevents us from making any substantial generalizations. Anyone who begins a sentence with the phrase "all religions ..." is certainly saying something false. It is therefore false to say that all religions are about private matters, belief, faith, the supernatural, spirituality, mystical experience, or anything else. Because the colloquial use of the word "religion" groups together so many dissimilar things, these generalizations are simply not true.

In addition, if the word "religion" groups together dissimilar things, there will not be anything that fundamentally distinguishes those things called religions from other sorts of cultural traditions. Consider the "sea creatures" example. We might try to make an essential distinction—"sea creatures are fundamentally different from land animals because the former breathe with gills and the latter breathe with lungs"—but it will not work, since the characteristics of both groups overlap: some sea creatures do, in fact, breathe with lungs, like some of the land animals. The same problem is true with "religions"—they cannot be essentially distinguished from other cultural traditions.

For instance, what is it that fundamentally distinguishes "religion" from "nationalism"? One might say that "nationalism" is concerned with *politics*, but "religion" is not, but that would be false: many of those traditions we call religious are extremely political. American evangelical Christians, for instance, are extremely politically active. One might say that nationalism concerns a *national territory*, but religions do not, but that would be false: some of those traditions we call religious are in fact linked to a territory or piece of land. Hindu nationalism is an important contemporary movement in India, and one that sees Hinduism as intrinsically linked to "Mother India" as a specific territory. One might say that nationalism doesn't have any *supernatural elements*, but religions do, but that too would be false: many forms of nationalism have supernatural elements. For instance, Hindu nationalism has a number of supernatural elements, as does American nationalism—as evidenced by the slogan "In God We Trust" on US money, and the inclusion of "one nation, under God" in the US pledge of allegiance. In the end, it turns out that there aren't really any fundamental differences between those things we colloquially call nationalisms and those things we colloquially call religions. There is no substantial reason to call the 4th of July a nationalist celebration as opposed to a religious one—the only reason why we call the 4th of July nationalist rather than religious is force of habit.

The colloquial use of the word "religion" is like the colloquial use of the word "furniture." There are no unique properties or characteristics that all things typically called "furniture" share. We can't make generalizations about "furniture," because it is a word that has a wide range of senses. We can't say all furniture is made out of wood. We can't say that all furniture is made out of fabric. In addition, there is nothing about "furniture" that fundamentally distinguishes it from other things one might find in a house. I'm looking at all the things in my living room: what makes my couch, my ottoman, and my TV stand "furniture," but not the curtains, the fireplace mantel, or the rug? Why does my bedroom dresser count as furniture, but not the kitchen cabinets? They both are made of wood, and they both are used for storage. Just like dressers and cabinets, "religion" and "nationalism" turn out to be very similar, and there isn't any fundamental distinction that can be made between the two.

In sum, our everyday application of the word "religion" is arbitrary and unsophisticated. As such, there is no way we could formulate a definition that will fit the colloquial use. This need not constitute a disaster—human beings get along every day using unsophisticated words. There is nothing wrong with utilizing the colloquial use, as long as we resist making generalizations about religion and avoid positing fundamental distinctions between "religion" and other types of cultural traditions.

Methods for Studying Religion

How should we approach the study of religion? One of the most common ways people study religion is based in their own religious tradition; we can call it the "my religion is true" approach. For instance, many conservative Christians are taught that Christian beliefs are true, and that other religious beliefs are false at best and demonic at worst. On this view, studying religion might amount to looking into how Christianity is true, how other religions are false, and how to convert people away from false religions. Many liberal Hindus are taught that all religions are *partially* true, because each particular religion is a branch on the same divine family tree—although it turns out that Hinduism tends to be *more true* than the other religions because it recognizes the underlying unity of all religions. On this view, studying religion might amount to looking for all the similarities each particular religion has, in order to prove they come from the same tree. The problem with these sorts of approaches is that they make far too many questionable assumptions: we cannot prove that all Christian beliefs are true, or that all religions are branches on the same divine tree. As such, these approaches and their related assumptions are inappropriate for academic or scholarly contexts.

A second common way people tend to think about religion is as a "belief system." On this view, religious practitioners subscribe to a system of beliefs, and the beliefs they hold inform or shape their behavior. For instance, many people believe that members of Al-Qaeda attacked New York City on 9/11 because they *believed* that there were seventy-two virgins, among other rewards, awaiting them in paradise. This theory of religion, however, simply does not work. As noted above, not all cultural traditions colloquially called religions focus on "beliefs," as this theory implies; some Zen practitioners even go so far as to say that beliefs are completely irrelevant. Second, even those who say beliefs are important rarely if ever have a *system* of beliefs—social and psychological research shows that people tend to hold a collection of contradictory beliefs that cannot be put together into a coherent system. In addition, research shows that people's behavior is often based on something other than their beliefs. Many people who *believe* they are not racist nevertheless *act* in extremely racist ways; similarly, many religious practitioners behave in ways that clearly contradict their stated beliefs. Finally, few religious practitioners fully subscribe to the apparently "official" beliefs of their religious tradition. For instance, most American Catholics support the use birth control despite the fact that official Catholic doctrine says it is immoral. The idea that religion is a belief system that directs practitioners' behavior collapses quickly under investigation. Despite the fact that many Americans hold that a

Muslim belief system made members of Al-Qaeda attack New York, studies have clearly demonstrated that their motivations were actually very complex, in addition to the fact that many Muslims with exactly the same religious beliefs actually oppose suicide terrorism (see Pape 2005). Beliefs are clearly *part of* those cultural institutions we call religions, but the evidence shows that beliefs are often contradictory, ignored, outright rejected, and so on—in which case the overly simple claim that "religion is a belief system" becomes nonsense. (We will return to this issue in Chapter 5.)

This book will therefore reject the "my religion is true" approach and the "belief system" approach; instead, we will approach the study of religion using what is called "functionalism" and a "hermeneutic of suspicion."

Functionalism and the Hermeneutics of Suspicion

Functionalism is relatively straightforward: scholars who use this approach look for a particular *function* religion might play in society. Although "hermeneutic of suspicion" is an unusual phrase, it too is relatively straightforward: the word "hermeneutic" is a technical term that means "method of interpretation," so a "hermeneutic of suspicion" is a *method of interpretation* that is *suspicious* of whatever is being studied. A hermeneutic of suspicion requires us, when faced with religious claims or religious practices, to approach those claims with scepticism. This is, in fact, what we do most of the time. Almost everyone is a sceptic; if we found ourselves faced with a murderer who says "God told me to do it," we would probably begin by doubting that claim and looking for other explanations or understandings of what is going on. We are liable to suggest, "perhaps he is schizophrenic," or "maybe he is using 'God' as an excuse for what he has done." (Of course, the same suspicion could be directed back at us: why would we assume that the gods *wouldn't* order someone to kill, especially when most religious traditions have stories about gods doing exactly that? Hermeneutics of suspicion are a double-edged sword; those who use it can have it turned back against them—and I'll have more to say about this below.)

Sigmund Freud's theory of religion is a perfect example of a functionalist approach joined with a hermeneutic of suspicion. Freud argued in *The Future of an Illusion* (1989) that all humans have desires or instincts that need to be repressed by society if society is to function. For instance, social order is maintained only on the condition that people repress their aggressive instincts and tendencies. However, for Freud, this repression takes an intolerably heavy toll on human psychology. Humans would not be able to handle this repression of their instincts were it not for some sort of psychological compensation to relieve the pressure. Freud believed that religion provides "illusions" that offer the sort of compensation or relief required. He argued that a religion like Christianity provides this psychological compensation through the creation of the illusion that adherents will go to heaven: human suffering in the present life can be indirectly relieved by the promise and hope that adherents will go somewhere perfect when they die. Why do religions exist? For Freud, the answer is simple: because something is necessary to alleviate the friction created by social repression. Religion in society is like the oil in an engine that keeps it from overheating.

It is important to note that Freud's understanding of religion is an outsider's view rather than an insider's. Scholars make a distinction between the view religious practitioners have of themselves (the insider's or "emic" view) and the view scholars have of them (the outsider's or "etic" view). If we asked a Christian what Christianity is all about, we would typically get an insider's view: God sent his son, Jesus Christ, to save human beings from sin by sacrificing himself on the cross. If we asked Freud, we would get something totally different—especially since he was suspicious of or sceptical about God, sin, or salvation. Freud would say that all of those things are illusions people believe in simply because they are necessary to relieve psychological pressure and thereby keep society running.

Freud's theory of religion is also called "reductionist" because he "reduces" religion to a psychological function; for him, religion can be completely explained away using the language of psychology. Christianity need not be understood as insiders understand it—the psychologist's outsider explanation of religion in psychological terms is sufficient in and of itself.

Bruce Lincoln, a functionalist who utilizes a hermeneutic of suspicion, argues that:

> The same destabilizing and irreverent questions one might ask of any speech act ought be posed of religious discourse. The

> first of these is "Who speaks here?", i.e., what person, group, or institution is responsible for a text, whatever its putative or apparent author. Beyond that, "To what audience? In what immediate and broader context? Through what system of mediations? With what interests?" And further, "Of what would the speaker(s) persuade the audience? What are the consequences if this project of persuasion should happen to succeed? Who wins what, and how much? Who, conversely, loses?" (Lincoln 1996, 226)

In focusing on these questions, he points out, we will "insist on discussing the temporal, contextual, situated, interested, human, and material dimensions of those discourses, practices, and institutions that characteristically represent themselves as eternal, transcendent, spiritual, and divine" (226). That is, whereas insiders will often describe their beliefs and their actions in terms of gods and goddesses, supernatural events, or eternal and transcendent values, if we use functionalism and a hermeneutic of suspicion we will explain their beliefs and actions in terms of historical contexts and material consequences. This form of functionalism translates (or "reduces") everything into social terms—as opposed to Freud, who reduces everything to psychology.

Using this approach does not mean that I am personally a sceptic about all things religious or that readers personally need to be sceptics—it just means that we will approach religious traditions *as if* we were sceptics *for the purpose of our study*. This means that when we come across insiders' claims about gods or goddesses, miracles, supernatural phenomena, or eternal truths, we will approach those claims with suspicion and distrust, and we will look for alternative descriptions or explanations of what's going on—particularly focusing on who benefits or who does not from these sorts of religious claims or practices. This element of the hermeneutics of suspicion is sometimes called "methodological atheism."

Methodological atheism is often misunderstood: people often assume that approaching religious traditions with suspicion or scepticism is unfair or cruel to religious people. However, this is not at all the case. Some scholars in the academic study of religion are very religious, but nevertheless approach their *academic studies* with this method. These scholars know that adopting this approach for their academic studies is not necessarily at odds with their religious faith or practice.

There are many scholars who are—for all practical purposes—atheists at work, but devout religious practitioners at home. In addition, they know that there are very good reasons for approaching the academic study of religion from this sceptical perspective.

In summary, this approach to the study of religion will first consider some cultural element—a myth, set of symbols, ritual, etc. Second, we will approach the material with suspicion and methodological atheism—we will assume for the sake of our study that any supernatural claims are false and will question what might motivate a group of practitioners to make such claims if they are not true. Finally, we will look for a functionalist explanation for the data under consideration—if this myth is not true, for instance, does it continue to be told because it serves some sort of social function for the community that tells it?

There are several reasons we can offer in support of functionalism and the hermeneutics of suspicion. The first reason for this approach is that, as we have already suggested, it turns out that almost everyone *already uses this method.* Even if one believes in the Christian god or the Muslim god, one probably does not believe in Ahura Mazda, or Asherah, or Chemosh. Everyone is an atheist *about someone else's gods*. Christians generally do not believe in Hindu gods; consequently, they tend to approach claims about what Hindu gods have done or said with a great deal of suspicion. Similarly, Jews and Muslims generally do not believe that Jesus was divine; consequently, they tend to approach Christian claims of Jesus' divinity with a great deal of suspicion. Everyone tends to be critical toward *other* religious traditions, but uncritical toward their own. Rather than be unfairly critical by excepting our own personal tradition from criticism while criticizing everyone else's, as scholars we should be *equally suspicious* toward all traditions.

A second reason for this approach—and this is probably the most important one—is that if we adopt a functionalist approach and a hermeneutic of suspicion, we will notice a number of interesting things we would not otherwise see. Consider the comic strip in Figure 1.1. Let's try to answer the question, "What's going on here?" If we are *not* suspicious, and we take the characters at their word, what's going on—from an insider's perspective—is that God apparently does not want this boy to eat candy. However, if we approach the question using a hermeneutic of suspicion, we will notice things we might not otherwise attend to. Perhaps what is going on—if we assume that gods don't

Figure 1.1 *Secret Asian Man* comic strip (© 2009 Tak Toyoshima, reproduced with permission).

exist—is that the father is appealing to the authority of divine beings to persuade his son not to eat candy. In fact, we might go on to notice that this is practically a universal phenomenon: "the gods want you to do this" often carries more authority—when it is persuasive—than "I want you to do this." If we assume a suspicious attitude toward claims about gods, we will more easily notice that saying "God wants you to do this" might function to *add authority to one's claims.*

Max Gluckman, an expert on indigenous African communities, provides us with a real example rather than a fictional one. He writes about how trading practices among Barotse communities are believed to develop supernatural properties; according to the insider's perspective,

> where a Barotse barters regularly with another they become "friends" and then perhaps "blood brothers"—quasi-kinsmen. Similarly, when a Barotse doctor treats a patient for a serious illness their relationship expands so that after the cure they are still "mystically" bound together by supra-sensible bonds, and, for example, if the patient does not pay him, the doctor's medicines will renew the illness. (Gluckman 1965, 78)

According to the Barotse, if an individual does not pay the doctor then the medicine given for the illness will magically make the illness return. However, from an outsider's perspective we can utilize a hermeneutic of suspicion and look for a functionalist explanation: if we assume that this claim is, in fact, *not true,* why might people in this community make such a claim? This one is easy to answer: if people believe this they will be more likely to pay their doctor's bills for fear of getting sicker. This is a myth that *serves the function of ensuring that doctors will be paid.*

Consider an example more relevant in North America: the Catholic Church officially insists that when priests pray over the bread and the wine—which is central to the ritual act of communion or the Eucharist—the bread literally turns into Jesus' body and the wine literally turns into Jesus' blood. In addition, the Church insists that *only* certified priests can do this—the magical saving power that is offered through the ritual will not work if administered by a priest who is not certified by the Catholic Church. Maybe this insider's claim is true and maybe it is not, but as scholars we can approach this using methodological atheism and look for a functionalist explanation. If we assume it is not true, what might be going on here? The answer is not obvious, but we can speculate that this belief and the associated practice is one that *serves the function of reinforcing the authority of the Catholic Church itself*. Catholics are told by the Church that they cannot go to other churches; the practice of communion in the other churches is *not real*—and therefore lacks any real power—because it is not administered by a Catholic priest. This claim—where it is persuasive—functions to protect the authority of the Church and make sure that practitioners do not leave the Catholic Church and go to other churches.

It is worth noting that this sort of functionalism is clearly reductionist: it reduces or translates "what is going on" into social terms. However, there is one very important way this reductionism is different from Freud's: we are not completely reducing religion to social terms. That is, we are not suggesting that religious traditions can be entirely explained in social terms without remainder. This is where strong reductionists such as Freud got into trouble: they showed how religious traditions could serve a particular psychological or social function, but then they went on to make the claim that religious traditions were *nothing more than that*. There are good reasons to think Freud's basic insight was partly correct: I am reminded of his argument every time I go to a Christian funeral, where I see people who comfort themselves and others in their grief by saying things like "we'll see her again when we get to heaven." It seems undeniable that religious traditions can be a part of psychological compensations for human suffering. Freud's problem was not that he pointed out that religious traditions could serve this psychological function, but that he said religious traditions did that and *nothing else*. The car engine metaphor I used above to describe Freud's theory was apt; strong functionalists have suggested that society works like a machine, and that religion is an essential part that has one and only one function in the machine. This has turned out to be false; religious traditions are far more complex and should not be reduced to only one function. As such, this book takes a *weak* functionalist approach—we will show how the elements of religious traditions can serve various social functions, but without completely reducing religion to those social functions.

The third reason in support of functionalism and a hermeneutic of suspicion is related to the previous one: even if our suspicion is unwarranted—that is, if it turns out that the supernatural claims under consideration *are true*—our functionalist explanation can still be true. To put it in other words, in many cases an insider's view and an outsider's functionalist explanation could both be true at the same time. I gave three examples above, and with each and every one of them, even if the supernatural explanations offered were true, our functionalist explanation of "what's going on" remains true as well:

1 Even if it is true that God doesn't want this boy to eat candy, *it is still true* that the father's appeal to the gods *functions to lend a special authority* to the claim that wouldn't be there if the father said "I don't want you to eat the candy."
2 Even if it is true that the Barotse doctor's medicines will make the patient sick if she does not pay, *it is still true* that this belief *functions to ensure that the doctor will be paid.*
3 Even if it is true that communion only works when it is administered by a priest certified by the Catholic Church, *it is still true* that this belief *functions to reinforce the central authority of the Catholic Church.*

A related issue is the fact that whenever scholars deal with religious traditions, they are almost always faced with competing and contradictory claims. As we will see in a later chapter, Christians have utilized the figure of Jesus to support a wide range of contradictory social and political positions. In fact, for just about any modern political position one could dream up (pro-capitalism, pro-communism, pro-life, pro-choice, progressive sexual norms, conservative sexual norms) we could find a book where Jesus has been said to support that position. However, it is not possible that Jesus could support all of those positions at once: some or most of these depictions of Jesus' social or political views *have to be false*. Of course, this poses no problem if we are using a hermeneutic of suspicion: it is easy to see, using this approach, that putting one's own values in Jesus' mouth gives them a special authority that they would not otherwise have. Since Jesus could not personally have supported all the values attributed to him, statistically speaking the sceptical functionalist explanation of what is going on—"these people are projecting their own values onto Jesus in order to make their views more authoritative"—is likely to be the right explanation *most of the time.*

A fourth reason we should use a hermeneutic of suspicion is that sometimes religious claims are demonstrably false. Religious practitioners often make claims that we can fact-check, and we sometimes find out that they have gotten the facts wrong. Christians once insisted that their god created the Earth and placed it at the center of the universe, and some still insist that the earth is only about 6,000 years old. But these beliefs are demonstrably false—the Earth is not at the center of the universe and it is much older than 6,000 years. Some Christians believe that the Bible is "literally true" in its entirety, but that is nonsense. Just ask them if they believe that it is "literally true" that Jesus is "the bread of life." Of course they don't think that—Jesus wasn't a baked good! Despite the popular claim that religion is always a matter of "faith"—and therefore beyond proof or disproof—religious practitioners often believe things that are demonstrably false, contradictory, or just plain nonsense, and these things both invite and deserve critical inquiry. All religious practitioners are human, and all humans make mistakes, make up stories, contradict themselves, and so on. When they do so, there is no reason to give them a free pass on their error just because the error was related to their "religion." As Lincoln (1996, 226) rightly suggests, "Reverence is a religious, and not a scholarly virtue. When good manners and good conscience cannot be reconciled, the demands of the latter ought to prevail."

Finally, we should utilize a hermeneutic of suspicion because every other academic discipline is suspicious of religious claims, and *we shouldn't give "religion" a special privilege we wouldn't give any other object of study*. Consider scientists: Galileo didn't turn away from a critical analysis of the solar system just because the Catholic Church told him that the Earth was at the center of the universe. On the contrary, he was sceptical of this claim—and his scepticism led him to important investigations that rightly challenged what the Church believed (eventually the Catholic Church came around to his point of view). Consider medicine: people once believed that when we sneeze we are expelling demons from our bodies. Thank goodness medical doctors didn't take this for granted and investigated into the ways in which allergies cause sneezing—if they hadn't challenged this nonsense we would not have allergy medicine. Consider historians: the history professors who work down the hall from me read stories all the time where historical events are attributed to the actions of gods, but that does not stop them from looking for other descriptions or explanations for these events. Academic disciplines are supposed to look for the truth, even when the truth challenges deeply held religious beliefs. Academics are not supposed to put up roadblocks that stop critical inquiry just because some religious group disagrees with their findings. Anthropologist Mary Douglas (1986, 24) puts it perfectly: "It does not help our understanding of religion to protect it from profane scrutiny by drawing a deferential border around it. Religion should not be exempted at all."

So we have five reasons we might want to use functionalism and a hermeneutic of suspicion. First, most people already use this method, except in an unfair way—they are uncritical toward their own tradition and critical toward others; by contrast, we should apply criticism evenly. Second, if we use this approach we are apt to notice things we might not otherwise notice, such as the fact that stories about gods often function to add authority to one's social agenda. Third, even if an insider's view turns out to be true, an outsider, functionalist explanation could also be true. Fourth, despite the popular but false idea that what we typically call religion is completely a matter of faith, we can sometimes prove that religious claims are false or contradictory. Finally, we should not give religion special privileges; like all other academic disciplines, the goal of religious studies should be to seek out the truth, even when it conflicts with people's religious beliefs.

This approach requires the same sort of scepticism employed by judges or jurors. Pretend you are on a jury for a case of attempted murder. Let's say that the alleged attempted murderer says he was *not* trying to kill anyone, but the alleged victim insists the defendant *was* trying to kill her. You, as a juror, cannot believe both at once. You will *have to be* suspicious. You might have to ask yourself questions like this: If the defendant is not telling the truth, what might he gain by lying? If the alleged victim is not telling the truth, what might she gain by lying? A hermeneutic of suspicion works the same way: if these claims about gods and goddesses cannot all be true, how might religious practitioners benefit by talking about gods and goddesses? By attending to these sorts of questions we will notice all sorts of things we wouldn't otherwise see. In sum, we are not using a hermeneutic of suspicion because no religious claims are true; we are employing this method because it is *useful*.

To summarize: the functionalism and hermeneutic of suspicion used in this book

- starts by considering what insiders say and do,
- remains suspicious or doubtful of all supernatural claims (methodological atheism),
- seeks to understand "what's going on" by reducing or translating religious claims or practices into social terms and social functions (reductionism and functionalism), while
- focusing on whose interests are served, but
- without suggesting that religious traditions can be *completely* reduced to one or more social functions (weak rather than strong functionalism), in order to
- discover things of interest that we might not otherwise notice.

Before moving on it is worth noting that functionalism and a hermeneutic of suspicion can be turned against those who use it. I encourage readers to be sceptical of the claims I make in this book. What might I seek to accomplish? Do I challenge or reinforce the status quo? Whose interests are advanced or undermined by the claims made?

Studying Religion versus Being Religious

Many insiders resist outsiders' critical study of their own religious tradition. No one likes their views and actions to be picked apart, as if under autopsy. Some object to the academic study of religion altogether. A critic of the academic study of religion once suggested that studying religion will not help people become religious; the critic used an interesting metaphor, comparing the study of religion to the study of birds: "no amount of theory can help an ornithologist to fly" (see Smith 2004, 208). Another scholar responded by saying, "Precisely! An ornithologist is not a bird *but one who studies birds*" (Smith 2004, 208; emphasis added).

Similarly, the point of religious studies is not to be religious but to study religion. On this view, one need not be religious to study religion, any more than one needs to be a bird to study birds, to be a plant to study plants, to be a Nazi to study Nazism, or to be sexist to study sexism. The last analogy is particularly instructive: there are lots of feminist scholars of religion who study how religious traditions are sexist—in doing so their goal is obviously not to be religious, but to criticize religions. Scholars are outsiders, not insiders. We will take it for granted that as scholars of religion our job is to study religions, understand how they work, and so on, *not* to advance religious agendas or convert people to a particular religious tradition.

However, by no means does it follow that this approach will be "neutral" between competing views. We noted above that many religious claims are demonstrably false. For instance, modern astronomy flatly contradicts the medieval Catholic Church's claim that the Earth is at the center of the universe (this, of course, led the Catholic Church to eventually revise its position on this matter). Our hermeneutic of suspicion will, in some cases, work against some religious claims or interests. I agree with Russell McCutcheon when he suggests that scholars should be "in the business of provoking unreflective participants in social systems into becoming reflective scholars of social systems" (McCutcheon 2001, 170). My goal is not to make readers more or less religious—my goal instead is to help them see how societies are constructed and maintained, especially when those societies contain oppression or domination. It would be silly to deny that this latter goal is, in many cases, at odds with the interests of, for instance, elites in patriarchal religious groups. Those feminists who study patriarchal religions are obviously not in the business of serving the interests of the patriarchs they study. In summary, religious piety is, in principle, separable from religious studies, and this book will be concerned with the latter rather than the former.

2

How Society Works: Classification

"A rose by any other name"?

William Shakespeare once wrote, "a rose by any other name would smell as sweet." The idea, of course, is that a thing is what it is, independently of the label placed on the thing. The process of labeling or naming is a secondary process, and one that does not change the nature of the thing named.

First → Second
Thing → Name/Label

If we found what we commonly call a rose in our flower garden and renamed it a "feces flower," that would not give the flower a foul smell. Changing the name does not change the thing itself.

Shakespeare's idea fits with common sense, but—as we will see—it is completely wrong much of the time. The most obvious counterexample to Shakespeare's claim is with respect to things like "money." Something is money only on the condition that a community recognizes it as money. If we cease to recognize a thing as money, it ceases to be money. Francs, which used to be money in France, are no longer recognized as money—the French have moved on to use euros. As such, francs are no longer money. Money by any other name *will not* be the same thing.

The reason for this is that some things are what they are not because of their material properties but because of a set of human social relations. In these cases, the relation between the thing and the human practice makes it what it is. Human categories often work similarly. One can be a "friend" not because of one's material make-up, but because of one's relationship to other humans. I am a "husband" because I have a partner who I married; if she died I would cease to be a husband and become a "widower." There is nothing about my physical make-up that makes me a husband or a widower—it is the *social relationship* between me and someone else. We are always in social contexts that determine who we are in ways that are relational: I was not a "professor" until my college hired me and made me one. You are not a "student" unless you are a student *of* someone or something.

Mary Douglas once similarly argued that there is nothing about the intrinsic material qualities of something that makes it "dirt." What makes something "dirt" is not its material constitution, but where it stands in relationship to humans. The drop of "soup" on my spoon is soup; the drop of soup on the floor is "dirt." The crumbs of bread on my plate are "crumbs"; the crumbs on the floor are "dirt." The hair on my head is just "hair"; the hair on the floor is "dirt." A common phrase gets at this point in a different way: "One person's trash is another's treasure." What makes something trash or treasure is not its intrinsic qualities, but its relationship to humans, human communities, or human interests.

Despite Shakespeare's insistence, sometimes what a thing is depends on the label given. What a "thing" is may *follow* rather than precede the name given to it. A copper disc *is* money *only when* it is given the name. In such cases, the label comes first, and what the thing is comes second. In these cases we have to reverse the model Shakespeare gave us above:

Second ← First
Thing ← Name/Label

Although a chapter on how language works might seem out of place in a book on religion and society, this subject matter is fundamental for two reasons. First, many important theorists—such as Émile Durkheim, Mary Douglas, Pierre Bourdieu, and J.Z. Smith—have argued that the way we classify or divide up the world is fundamental to understanding how religious traditions function to reinforce social order. This chapter will consider how classification works according to the theory of social constructionism, and Chapter 5 will connect classification more clearly with religious traditions and the reproduction of social order. Second, most of us inherit the sort of common-sense view of language and the world assumed by Shakespeare, but because of the sorts of reasons we will consider below, this view started to be rejected by philosophers in the eighteenth century and became widely rejected by all critical scholars in the twentieth century (whether in philosophy, religious studies, history, sociology, etc.). Getting past the common-sense view of language is the first step to high-quality, critical scholarship, and all of the remaining chapters of this book assume the view of language presented in this chapter.

Words Create Worlds

The basic idea of social constructionism is that we, as humans, make the world what it is for us. The world is not just there for us to find and discover—rather, we make the world what it is through our use of language. Philosopher Hilary Putnam provides a great example of how this works (see Putnam 2004, 38ff). How many things are in the box in Figure 2.1? An obvious response, of course, is *three*. However, as Putnam goes on to point out, this answer only makes sense if we are counting in a particular way. We could count other "things" in the box. How many *possible pairs* of circles are there? *Three*. How many *possible groups of three* circles are there? *One*. How many "things" are there if we add circles and groups of circles? *Seven*. How many square inches of white space are there? How many molecules of black ink are there?

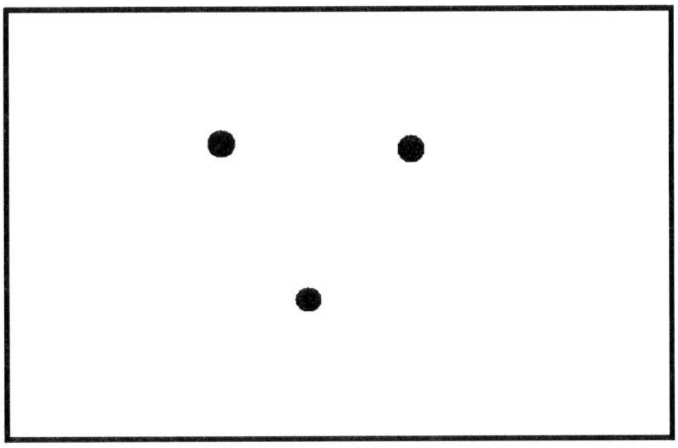

Figure 2.1 How many things are in the box?

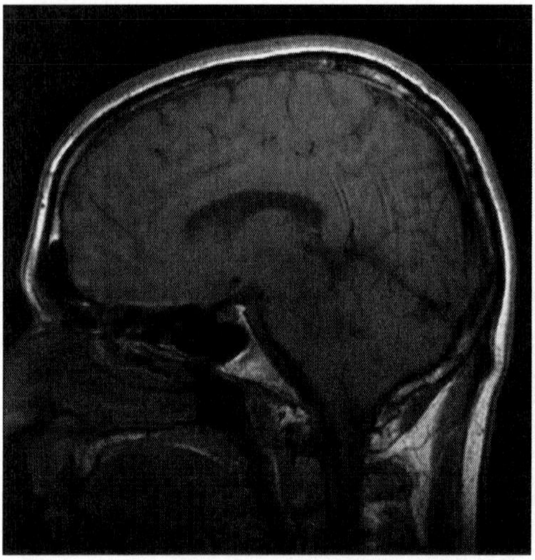

Figure 2.2 MRI scan (Creative Commons Copyright (cc) erat).

We could go on and on, of course, but the problem is clear: how many "things" there are in the box depends on how we are counting.

If a doctor looks at a human body using an MRI machine and an X-ray machine she will see completely different things (Figures 2.2 and 2.3). What tools we use to "see" make up what we see. For social constructionists, the same thing is true of everything in the world—the *concepts* we use to "see" the world make up what we see. A political scientist could come into my classroom and, using a particular set of concepts, find 45 percent Republicans, 45 percent Democrats, and 10 percent unaffiliated. A religion scholar could come into my classroom and, using a different set of concepts, find 80 percent Christians, 10 percent Jewish, and 10 percent unaffiliated. A chemist could come into my classroom and may find certain percentages of oxygen, nitrogen, etc., in the air. What the world looks like to them—what they see—depends on what concepts they use to look at the world.

Some readers were no doubt unconvinced above: "there are only three things in the box—a 'group' isn't a thing." But this clearly will not work. All concepts *group together* stuff in the world. The "head" in the picture above is a *grouping* of a skull, a brain, blood vessels, facial muscles, nasal cavities, etc. The "brain" itself is a *grouping* of brain matter, nerves, blood vessels, etc. Even the "circles" in the box are *groupings* of

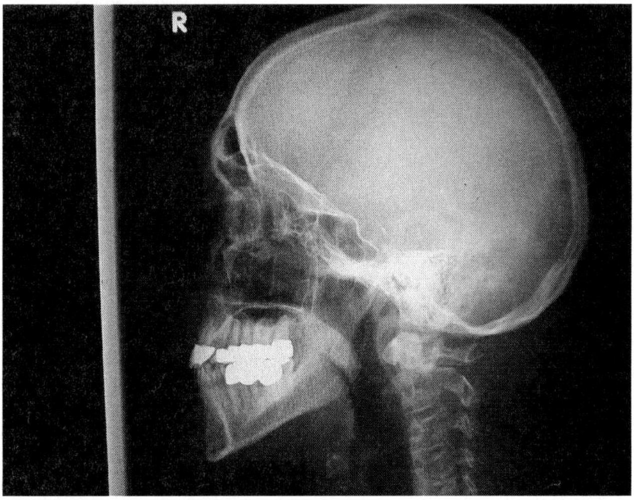

Figure 2.3 X-ray image (Creative Commons Copyright (cc) erix!).

ink molecules in a particular formation. (The only things in the universe that might not be groupings would be subatomic particles, and no one has ever seen those—they are products of scientific hypotheses.) "Things" are not just there as things in the world—our concepts "group" stuff and *only then* is that stuff there for us as "things."

To my knowledge, the best example is to think of the stuff of the world like a roll of cookie dough (see Figure 2.4). What cookies are contained therein? Of course that depends on what cookie cutters we select. For all practical purposes, we can consider concepts as cookie cutters: with them we bring into relief the stuff of the world for us. If we use different concepts, we get different results. Also consider the image on the cover of this book: the constellations we pull out from among the various stars in the sky depend on what interests us. The Greeks and Romans pulled out figures such as Orion, Cancer, and Cassiopeia, but this Christian artist—Andreas Cellarius, who first published the cover image in his 1660 volume *Harmonia Macrocosmica*—pulled out saints, Noah's ark, and the Ark of the Covenant. These are not the same constellations with different names—they are altogether different groupings based on different interests.

The categories we use are almost always directly linked to our human interests. Rodney Needham puts it well:

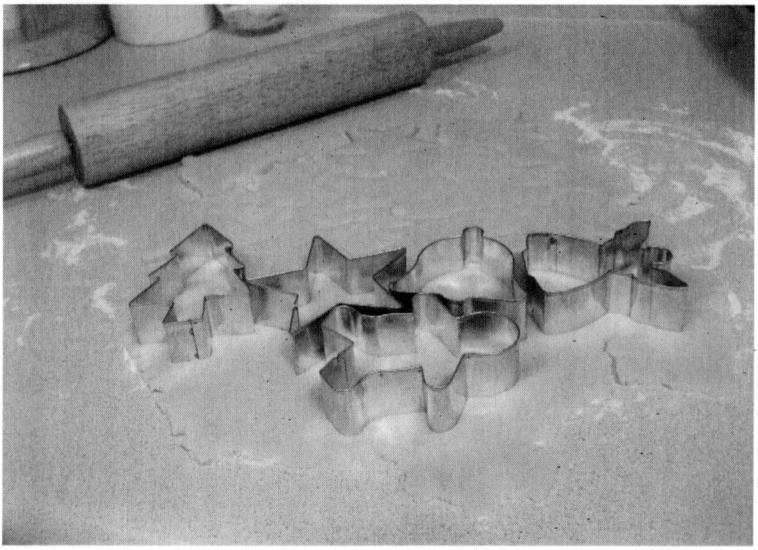

Figure 2.4 Cookie dough (Creative Commons Copyright (cc) SarahInDisguise).

> in order to think about the world, and also to act upon it, we need to divide phenomena into classes. We have to group things together according to what we think are significant resemblances as, for example, when we discriminate a class of objects as edible mushrooms. And we need to distinguish a contrasted class by significant difference, as when we circumscribe a further class of objects as poisonous mushrooms. (Needham 1979, 17)

What is important is that it is *we* who divided mushrooms that way. Mushrooms do not appear to us in the world in those two categories: *we* are the ones dividing them into categories, and for *our* purposes. In addition, if we change our interests our categories may change as well. When I was young I was allergic to all nuts *except* peanuts and almonds. Consequently, my family made a distinction between that category of nuts ("the safe ones") and all the other ones ("the bad ones"). There was nothing natural about that distinction—it resulted merely from my family's concerns. Families without such allergies would have no use for this classification. Classification is always linked to human interests in some way or other.

There are seven key principles to social constructionism, and we already have the first two. First principle: *words are tools that humans use to delimit from the stuff of the world what is of interest to them*. Second principle: *the tools we use produce the world for us; if we used a different set of tools, we would have a different world*, just the same as if we used a different set of cookie cutters, we would have different cookies.

The third principle of social construction is that *the uses of words are variable*. For instance, the way people use the word leprosy today is different from the way it was used 2,000 years ago; back then, the word was used to pick out a number of kinds of skin diseases. Consequently, when we read about Jesus healing "lepers" in the New Testament, the author may not be talking about the same thing we mean when we think of lepers—perhaps those "lepers" just had psoriasis.

The fourth principle is that *variable uses are all we have—there are no intrinsically right or wrong uses of words, just different uses*. If what is counted as a leper depends on the specific use of the word in a particular context, and if there are no right or wrong uses, it would be nonsensical to ask what a leper "really is." Asking what a leper "really is" would be tantamount to asking how the word leper is used outside of any particular social context, or asking how the word is used when no one is using it. From a social constructionist perspective, rather than ask what a leper really is, what is important is figuring out exactly how we and others use or have used the word in specific contexts.

Consider how these four principles bear on our understanding of the use of the word "planet." In 2006, a team of astronomers at the International Astronomical Union voted to change the definition of the term "planet," such that Pluto no longer fitted the definition, and would no longer officially be considered a planet. The purpose behind this definitional change was the simplification of the taxonomy of astronomical objects: astronomers have found objects in the solar system bigger than Pluto—it was apparently easier for them to narrow the definition of a "planet," such that it excluded Pluto, rather than to call all of these newly found objects "planets" as well. Among the scientific communities that view this union as authoritative, Pluto is now considered a "dwarf planet," rather than a "planet."

Now, if we had a time machine, and one of these astronomers from 2006 went back in time to 2005, it is possible that she might get into an argument with a 2005 astronomer about Pluto's status. Our friend from 2006 could claim that Pluto is not a planet, and our astronomer from 2005 might well claim that that is absurd. There may be no disagreement about what Pluto looks like, what Pluto is made of, its mass, its orbit, its gravity, etc. One would hope that the differences between them would be resolved were they to find that each is using a different definition of "planet," and a different taxonomy of astronomical objects. Presumably, their argument would end with the sudden realization: "Oh, you're using the term 'planet' differently than I am." These two astronomers need not establish what a planet "really is." Indeed, what could that even mean? To understand each other, our astronomers only need to establish clearly how each is using the term.

Similarly, people often argue about what religion really is; but if social constructionism is right, this is a silly argument. Realizing this would rectify a number of confusions. People frequently get into heated debates over whether Buddhism is "really" a religion. However, rather than pose the question "is Buddhism a religion?," it would be beneficial to change the question slightly and ask whether Buddhism counts as religion, given this or that specific use of the term religion. On some definitions of religion, Buddhism will be a religion; on other definitions of religion, Buddhism will not be. If the principles of social constructionism are correct, there is no need to determine whether Buddhism is *really* a religion, any more than our astronomers from 2005 and 2006 need to determine whether Pluto is *really* a planet—this sort of inquiry would be rendered nonsensical. This task would be replaced with the endeavor to be clear about the different ways these terms are used. We might, of course, disagree about which definitions are ultimately more useful, but this is a pragmatic matter: which definition is more useful for such and such context, given such and such purposes? Edward Schiappa puts it this way:

> Instead of posing questions in the time-honored manner of "What is X?" ([such as] "What is a planet?," "What is a terrorist?," "What are sexual relations?"), I suggest that we reformulate the matter as "How *ought* we use the word X?" given our particular reasons for defining X. (Schiappa 2003, xi)

The discussion that would follow the last question would be much more clear and navigable than the one that would follow the question about whether Buddhism is "really" a religion.

People often conclude from the fourth principle that anything can be true and that nothing can be false for a social constructionist, but that is not true at all. If we have agreed to use the old definition of "planet," then Pluto *is* a planet. If we have agreed to use the new definition of "planet," then Pluto *is not* a planet. Social constructionism does not suggest that "anything goes"; it suggests that when determining whether a claim is true we will have to carefully attend to the definitions our community is using, and the truth or falsity of the claim will only extend as far as our community (or other communities using the same concepts in the same way). For this reason, the fifth principle of social constructionism is that *although the uses of words change, this does not mean that anything is true—whether a claim is true depends on the agreed use of the words for a particular community.*

When we change the concepts we use, we bring into relief different things from the world—changing a concept is like using another cookie cutter to slice up dough. However, it would be silly to think that changing the concepts we use always changes the world as it is. Pluto is indifferent to the concepts we use to bring it into relief—we can call it a planet, a dwarf planet, an asteroid, or a hemorrhoid, and that will have no effect on its mass, gravity, orbit, atmosphere, etc. The properties of Pluto do not change when we change its name. However, the same thing is not at all true of humans. Our properties *do* change if we categorize ourselves differently.

This is the sixth principle of social constructionism: *what we are as humans is a result or product of the concepts and practices in our societies.* I am all of the following:

- a doctor (of philosophy, not medicine),
- a guitar player,
- a football fan,
- a driver,
- an internet user,
- a reader,
- a voter,
- a citizen, and
- a professor.

All of those things that I am only make sense because I live in a particular type of society—I could not be any of these if I grew up as a caveman. From a social constructionist perspective, we, as humans, are a *product* of society. I cannot be a king in my society, although I could be a president. Similarly, a man in fifteenth-century Europe couldn't be a president, although he could be a king. Kings and presidents are what they are *only because* there is a social system set up to recognize those social roles. No society, no kings. No society, no professors. No society, no college students. I cannot emphasize this enough: we are what we are because society makes us that way—*humans are products of societies.*

This point deserves emphasis because we tend to forget it. Usually, we take it for granted that we just are what we are; we assume that our identities are natural features of the world. But the social constructionist insists: there's nothing natural about it—*our identities are social.* Calling Pluto a dwarf planet does not change Pluto, but calling someone a president instead of a king *would change* him. Because humans can respond to what they're called, there's a circular effect between what we are called and what we are. We organize ourselves in response to what we call ourselves:

> The responsiveness to new labels suggests extraordinary readiness to fall into new slots and to let selfhood be redefined. This is not like the naming that … creates a particular version of the world by picking out certain sorts of things, for instance, naming stars, foregrounding some and letting others disappear from sight. *It is a much more dynamic process by which new names are uttered and forthwith new creatures corresponding to them emerge.* (Douglas 1986, 100; emphasis added)

Louis Althusser calls this "hailing": we are "hailed" by others and, in responding to hails, become what we are called (Althusser 2008, 44ff). Ian Hacking calls it "making up people": "human beings … come into being hand in hand with our invention of the ways to name them" (Hacking 2002, 113). Whatever we call it, philosophers, anthropologists, sociologists, and social theorists across disciplines agree that what humans are is not established prior to the advent of the classifications and labels we use to sort humans into different categories.

This is even true of human groups organized around such seemingly natural traits as race, sex, hair color, etc. There was once a famous experiment where a 3rd grade teacher divided her class between brown-eyed and blue-eyed students:

> On the first day, the blue-eyed children were told they were smarter, nicer, neater, and better than those with brown eyes. Throughout the day, [Jane] Elliott [the teacher] praised them and allowed them privileges such as a taking a longer recess and being first in the lunch line. In contrast, the brown-eyed children had to wear collars around their necks and their behavior and performance were criticized and ridiculed by Elliott. On the second day, the roles were reversed and the blue-eyed children were made to feel inferior while the brown eyes were designated the dominant group.
>
> What happened over the course of the unique two-day exercise astonished both students and teacher. On both days, children who were designated as inferior took on the look and behavior of genuinely inferior students, performing poorly on tests and other work. In contrast, the "superior" students—students who had been sweet and tolerant before the exercise—became mean-spirited and seemed to like discriminating against the "inferior" group. (Frontline 1985)

Of course the teacher did not make her students have blue eyes or brown eyes, but the teacher did teach the students to organize themselves around these categories. There is nothing natural about privileging those particular categories: we could organize human groups around height, weight, hair color, hair length, skin color, clothing, and so on. There is no intrinsic reason for us to privilege one set of categories over another, except for particular purposes (perhaps we want to divide people by height when we are taking a group picture, so the tall ones do not cover up the short ones). Judith Lorber notes,

> in Western societies, we see two discrete sexes and two distinguishable genders because our society is built on two classes of people, women and men. Practically every form you fill out asks whether you are male or female, even though your psychology or biology may be irrelevant for what the form is used for. (Lorber 1994, 38)

It might make sense to emphasize the difference between male and female for the purposes of sexual reproduction, but we segregate according to sex even when what we are doing has nothing to do with reproduction. I know of no one who has tried to conceive a child while in a public restroom, but for some reason our society separates bathrooms for men and women. Why divide restrooms by sex rather than by size, age, ability (i.e., divide for able-bodied and handicapped individuals), or group type (i.e., divide for adult individuals and adults with children)? The last two ways of sorting would be much more practical.

As Pierre Bourdieu notes in his discussion of rite of passage rituals for males (such as ritual circumcisions that take place at the onset of puberty),

> [this ritual] says: this man is a man—implying that he is a real man, which is not always immediately obvious. It tends to make the smallest, weakest, in short, the most effeminate man, separated by a difference in nature and essence from the most masculine woman, the tallest, strongest woman, etc. To instate, in this case, is to consecrate, that is, to sanction and sanctify a particular state of things, an established order, in exactly the way that a constitution does in the legal and political sense of the term. An *investiture* (of a knight, Deputy, President of the Republic, etc.) consists of sanctioning and sanctifying a difference (pre-existent or not) by making it *known* and *recognized*; it consists of making it exist as a social difference, known and recognized as such by the agent invested and everyone else. (Bourdieu 1999, 119)

Social rituals (and social practices in general) invest the most insignificant natural differences with an incredible social significance. Blue eyes or brown eyes, white skin or dark skin, and so on: these are not socially significant in and of themselves; they become significant when they are socially constructed as such. Shared ways of thinking "assign disparate items to classes and load them with moral and political content" (Douglas 1986, 63). And social consequences almost always follow from assigning an individual to a class or category.

We tend to think of language as *mapping* the world around us. The world is just there, and we draw a map tracing its outlines. This was basically Shakespeare's view when he said "a rose is a rose." However, for social constructionism, this is terribly false and misleading, especially when it comes to social facts. Our concepts do not map the social world—they are *blueprints* for the social world. In the United States, there is a president, a supreme court, a congress, and so on. The concepts "president," "judge," and so on do not map a pre-existing system, they *create* the system. Americans could not have their political system without that set of concepts, which constitutes the blueprint of the social world they live in.

Here we are circling back to where we began: the penny in my pocket is money only because I live in a society where people believe, as a part of a mutual agreement, that it is a legitimate form of currency. Because we believe this, it actually *is* a legitimate form of currency. Even though it is a social fact rather than a natural fact that euros rather than francs are legitimate currency at this time in France, there is nothing unreal or untrue about this. The common-sense idea that something is true or false independently of human beliefs or human conventions does not work; whether something is true or false necessarily results in part from a particular relationship between the stuff of the world and human beliefs and conventions. A hair on my head is a hair, but when it falls on the floor it becomes dirt. Of course nothing about the hair is materially changing, but its status *for us* changes. What makes it go from being just hair to being dirt is its *relationship to a human community*.

So we have the seventh principle of social constructionism: *social facts, although social, are nevertheless real facts—if only for the community that recognizes them as such*. The last part of the principle is an important qualification—my dollar bill *really is* legitimate currency, but only for those communities that recognize it as such. My dollar bill may cease to be legitimate currency if I leave America and travel to a country that will not accept US currency.

This last principle is tricky because people within communities almost never completely agree about their system of classification. Philosopher Chiara Bottici notes:

> In the case of social entities such as nations, classes, and states, we are not dealing simply with abstract notions, but with socially constructed beings: it is because there are narrating bodies [i.e., communities of individuals that tell stories about them] that behave *as if* such beings existed, that they do *actually* exist. (Bottici 2007, 241)

However, there are almost always *multiple* stories or narratives about nations and states, and it is not always possible to combine them into a common narrative or common identity. As a result, "the plurality of stories may turn into the recognition that *there is no common story* to be told" (Bottici 2007, 242; emphasis added).

Today, the United States is no longer a colony of Great Britain. However, was it independent on July 4th, 1776, the day the Declaration of Independence was signed? It *was* independent of Great Britain in the minds of the Americans who signed, but it certainly *was not* independent in the minds of King George III and most British citizens. The recognition of America's "independence" was at first recognized by some but not others, and only several years later did it come to be recognized by all. And often there is *never* a universal recognition of a social fact, in which case it seems that it never entirely becomes a "fact." Although to my knowledge everyone today recognizes America's independence from Great Britain, there are different stories to be told about places in the world like Palestine or Kashmir, over which people continue to fight. "[T]here is never the guarantee that all these stories can be reconciled into a single plot" (Bottici 2007, 245).

An Important Example

In modern Western culture, one can be one of only two sexes: male or female. We usually take this to be a straightforward, natural, biological fact, but things are not that simple. Considering how social constructionists think about the seemingly simple distinction between male and female will shed light on how valuable (and how radical) social constructionism really is.

1 Words are tools that humans use to delimit from the stuff of the world what is of interest to them

Whether or not one is "male" or "female" is of considerable interest to most people in our society, particularly because—for better or for worse—we tend to treat people differently based on how we identify their sex. When we meet new people, their sex is often one of the first things we notice.

2 The tools we use produce the world for us; if we used a different set of tools, we would have a different world

The male/female distinction has been the dominant one throughout human history, but it is not the only one. Some cultures have *three* sexes, rather than two (and a feminist biologist once suggested that it would be useful to recognize five sexes in our own culture—male, female, and three types of hermaphrodites in between; see Fausto-Sterling 1993). Our society would be very different if we divided people up into three sexes. Sexual preferences would multiply: there wouldn't be just heterosexual, homosexual, and bisexual—we would have to create a range of new categories, such as trisexual. Dating rituals and sexed social codes (such as the current practice of the male proposing to the female) would change and get a lot more complicated.

3 The uses of words are variable. The way in which people have used the words "male" and "female" has changed over time

One great example is found in Anne Fausto-Sterling's book, *Sexing the Body*. There she points out that for the Olympics there is a sexual division for each event—men are not allowed to compete with women. But how do they decide whether someone is a man or a woman? In the past they would line everyone up before a panel of judges and require them to pull down their pants—those individuals with penises competed as males and those individuals with vaginas competed as women. However, the people who run the Olympics changed their system several years ago, presumably because they thought forcing participants to strip was too invasive. Instead, they switched over to doing DNA tests: those individuals with XY genes competed as men and those individuals with XX genes competed as women (see Fausto-Sterling 2000, 1–3).

So, what's the difference? *Not everyone with XX genes has "female" genitalia, and vice versa.* Studies estimate that 1½ to 2 percent of the human population has genitalia that do not match up to their DNA the way most people think they would (Fausto-Sterling 2000, 51–3; see also Butler 1990, 106–11). In a college class of 30 to 50 students, it is more likely than not that there is an "intersexed" person in the class. There are about 1,200 to 1,400 students at my college; that means there are probably 20 or 25 intersexed students on campus. Several years ago there was a "woman" ("she" had "female" genitalia) who, surprisingly, discovered after her DNA test that "she" had XY genes. As a result, "she" was disqualified from competing as a woman (Fausto-Sterling 2000, 1–3). The use of words is variable: on the old system, the Olympic Committee would have categorized this individual as a "woman," but on the present system the Olympic Committee categorized this individual as a "man." Whether one is identified as a male or female depends on what way we decide to sort out the differences between male and female. On one system of classification an individual might be female, but on another she might be male. And if we had three sexes instead of just two, one might be neither.

As Ian Hacking rightly notes, our uses of classifications and categories are constantly shifting:

> New slots [are] created in which to fit and enumerate people. Even national and provincial censuses amazingly show that the categories into which people fall change every ten years. Social change creates new categories of people, but the counting is no mere report of developments. It elaborately … creates new ways for people to be. (Hacking 2002, 100)

4 Variable uses of words are all we have—there are no intrinsically right or wrong uses of words, just different uses

There seems to be no reason to say that one way of defining sex is the right way.

5 Although the uses of words change, this does not mean that everything is true—whether a claim is true depends on the agreed-upon use of the words for a particular community

Just because the way sex is determined is variable does not mean that anything goes. If our operative definition of "male" is "has a penis," then even if an individual with a penis has XX genes or wants to be identified, as female, he will be male *for this given definition*. However, if our operative definition of male is "has XY genes," then she will be female *for that definition*. What is true will depend on what classification system we have in place.

6 What we are as humans is a result of the concepts and practices in our societies

This is true when it comes to sex in at least three ways. First, if I were born in a society that had three sexes, I might not be male, so my male identity is, in part, a product of the concepts my society uses.

Second, identities carry rights and privileges in societies. It is pretty clear that whether one is identified as male or female has a great deal to do with the rights and duties assigned to one in our society. The woman/man who wanted to compete as a woman, but couldn't because she/he had "male" DNA, was stripped of some rights and duties and assigned an alternative set once her DNA was determined. These rights and privileges become a part of our identity. Who we *are*, socially speaking, is a product of the rights and responsibilities assigned to us by our communities.

Third, as Judith Lorber notes,

> there is ample evidence that once gender is assigned, boy and girl children are handled and reacted to quite differently.
>
> Take the phenomenon of boys' boisterousness or girls' physical awkwardness in Western societies. When little boys run around noisily, we say "Boys will be boys" …. But are boys, universally, the world over, in every social group, a vociferous, active presence? Or just where they are encouraged to use their bodies freely, to cover space, take risks, and play outdoors at all kinds of games and sports? Conversely, what do we mean when we say, "She throws like a girl"? … In fact, she throws like a person who has already been taught to restrict her movements, to protect her body, to use it femininely.
>
> (Lorber 1994, 39–40)

Just as parents tend to encourage boys to behave in certain ways, so girls are discouraged (and vice versa). During our childhood, most of us heard our parents say—innumerable times—"boys don't do that" or "girls don't do that." Because of this, scholars have begun talking about sex and gender as analogous to muscle memory: we are habituated to behave in certain sexually different ways until they become natural to us, although there is nothing natural about these behaviors to begin with. As a result, who we are or who we become, as far as our sexual and gendered identities are concerned, is a product of the practices in our societies.

7 Social facts, although social, are nevertheless real facts—if only for the community that recognizes them as such

Things in the world are what they are because we identify them as such. Although this man's genitalia didn't change when he began to be called a man by the Olympic Committee, it nevertheless remains a fact that on the Olympic Committee's criterion, he was a man. That it was a social fact does not make it any less of a fact, although its truth *extends only as far* as those communities that share the committee's definition of male and female. For communities with a different criterion (such as the *old* Olympic Committee), he would, as a matter of fact, have been a woman.

The social construction of something like a "college" is fairly easy to understand: without a community who recognized these roles, we couldn't have a president, a dean, professors, students, etc. By contrast, understanding the social construction of something like sex or race is much trickier. One's sex or race seems natural, rather than social—but this is only because we forget (or never noticed) that people have divided up the sexes and the races in different ways at different times. As a result, we misrecognize social categories by taking them as merely or simply natural categories. As Bourdieu rightly notes, the practice of sorting people into apparently natural categories "is an act of social magic that can create difference … by exploiting as it were pre-existing differences. … The distinctions that are the most efficacious socially are those which give the appearance of being based on objective differences" (Bourdieu 1999, 120). Consider the teacher mentioned above who divided her students between blue-eyed and brown-eyed students: this is exactly what Bourdieu is talking about. There is something seemingly "natural" about the distinction—clearly there are some students with blue eyes and some with brown eyes. This "natural" difference lent a certain credibility to the social grouping of students, although the social effects of that particular grouping were far from warranted. Social rituals (and social practices in general) invest the most insignificant natural differences with an incredible social significance. Once constructed, social categories tend to take on a life of their own. When they do this, and when their constructed nature is made to appear as if it were natural—for example, religious traditions often suggest sex binaries were divinely ordained—this is called "naturalization," a concept we will discuss further below.

Animism and Essentialism

Long ago, before people had a better understanding of what we today call natural phenomena, people projected spirits, gods, or goddesses behind natural phenomena. What causes thunder? There must be a thunder god. What causes rain? There must be a rain god. If there was a phenomenon one could not understand, one could project an animating spirit behind the phenomenon to explain it. This projection of spirits or gods behind natural phenomena is what is referred to as *animism*.

Cognitive scientists argue that all humans, even today, have the tendency toward animism, or the tendency to project agency where there is none (see Boyer 2002). Animism is very much alive and well today, although we do not usually refer to it as such. Today scholars call it "essentialism." What is essentialism? Let me begin with an example. Probably one of the most obvious examples of essentialism in our recent history has been race essentialism. Throughout the nineteenth century, many white Americans presumed that there was some sort of essence that all African-Americans had in common—some sort of black essence that was inferior, of course, to the essence that white people had in common. Of course, such essences could not be seen—if one dissected white and black corpses one would not be able to find some sort of essence, hidden deep inside the body. Nevertheless, it was widely believed that all black people shared the same black essence, and all white people shared the same white essence.

We also see this today when it comes to talk about gender. It is presumed that all women have identical essences, and men have identical essences. "Men are from Mars and women are from Venus," as the saying goes. This follows only if men and women have different essences that determine their behavior in different ways.

Essentialism works like this: first a label is attached to something, and then an essence is projected behind the label. On the basis of the essence, additional characteristics are attributed to whomever carries that label, and various social roles are often prescribed. Consider a superficial example: the application of the label "blonde." If someone is blonde, perhaps we can project an essence on that person—there must be something intrinsically or essentially *dumb* about that person. From that we can attribute additional characteristics, and then assign a social role: because blonde people are not smart, they will make mistakes on the job, and as such we should avoid giving them any real responsibility at work. The first step is to assign a label, project an essence behind the label, and the other things follow from there:

Projected hidden essence	←	Label	→	Additional characteristics	→	Social role
Dumbness	←	Blonde	→	Will make mistakes	→	Do not give responsibility

This is, of course, a very silly example—to my knowledge no one takes seriously the idea that blondes are intrinsically dumb and need to be treated as such. However, in the past being placed in the category of "black" had very serious additional characteristics attributed, as well as social roles assigned, such as "slave." Until very recently those individuals slotted into the category of "woman" had a hidden essence projected onto them, on the basis of which additional characteristics such as "isn't smart enough for politics" were attributed—consequently, they were denied the right to vote. Even today the category of "woman" often involves the attribution of characteristics such as "weak," along with the behavioral recommendation that "women should be protected by their men"—despite the fact that there are a lot of women in the world who are stronger than a lot of men, and we do not recommend that weak men need to be protected by stronger men. The attribution of additional characteristics and behaviors, roles, and privileges on the basis of a classification alone is almost never reasonable.

All of this is, of course, a more precise way of talking about stereotypes. If we label someone as a part of a group, we often project the characteristics presumed to belong to the group on the individual in question, whether or not that individual has those general characteristics. Consider the belief that "women are weaker and more emotional than men"—some people take this to be the case *even if* they know that some women are, in fact, stronger and less emotional than some men (we usually do not let matters of fact get in the way of our stereotypes).

No doubt some readers are wondering why we are so far from those cultural traditions we call religions. But all of this has everything to do with religion. Religious traditions are often centrally concerned with creating and assigning categories of persons and projecting essences. For instance, in the Bhagavad Gita—an ancient Hindu text—the god Krishna tells Arjuna the following:

> The actions of priests, warriors,
> commoners, and servants
> are apportioned by qualities
> born of their intrinsic being.
>
> Tranquility, control, penance,
> purity, patience and honesty,
> knowledge, judgment, and piety
> are intrinsic to the action of a priest.
>
> Heroism, fiery energy, resolve,
> skill, refusal to retreat in battle,
> charity, and majesty in conduct
> are intrinsic to the action of a warrior.
>
> Farming, herding cattle, and commerce
> are intrinsic to the action of a commoner;
> action that is essentially service
> is intrinsic to the servant.
>
> Each one achieves success
> by focusing on his own action;
> hear how one finds success
> by focusing on his own action.
>
> (Miller 1986, 141)

Here Krishna is saying that those born in each of the four classes have an essence (which he calls their "intrinsic being"), from which it follows that we can attribute additional characteristics and a social role:

Warrior's "intrinsic being"	←	Warrior	→	Heroic, energetic, etc.	→	Social role of soldier

For anyone born into the warrior class we can project a warrior's essence. Because of the warrior essence, we can attribute additional characteristics, and ones that will make those in this class suitable for the social role of a soldier or fighter. This projected essence is merely projected, of course—there have been people born in the warrior class who do not, in fact, possess all the qualities attributed to them (as a result, they were probably not particularly well-suited to the social role assigned to them). In the end, this sort of attribution of an essence works in the same way as racism.

As anthropologist Rodney Needham rightly suggests,

> An individual, in being associated with one of these divisions, participated in all the other members of that symbolic class; his character and his destiny are determined by it. The members of a division in this classification were ... thought of as constituting a unity. (Needham 1979, 11)

For Needham, one's destiny is determined by one's class *not* in the sense of having an essence that determines one's behavior, but rather in the sense that *the community determines one's destiny* on the basis of the identity they assign: rights and duties are assigned on the basis of one's category or class (Needham 1979, 21). Once this sort of animism or essentialism is engaged, there is little one can do to escape from it.

Perhaps there would be nothing wrong with using categories in this way if all things in a category really were identical. All "sharp knives" are good for cutting simply because they are in the group of things that are "sharp." The assignment of a use on the basis of the category makes sense in this sort of case.

> In the traditional definition of a class in western philosophy, its members share at least one common feature; it is by virtue of this point of resemblance that the individuals belong to the class. At its logical extreme this definition is taken to mean that the principle of substitution will apply: i.e., that whatever we know of one object in a class we know of other objects, to the extent that they are alike. For a great many practical purposes, this common-feature definition of a class is appropriate and useful. Once we classify a thing as a knife we may assume that it can be put to use in certain ways that a fork could not.

> What we know about one carburetor we know, by and large, about any other carburetor; they may not be identical, or interchangeable, but we can at least get a conceptual grasp on them and understand where they fit. (Needham 1979, 63)

The problem, of course, is that the same is not at all true of classes of humans:

> In other cases—probably in the majority—the ethnographic evidence provides no reason to think that the members of a symbolic class are connected by features that are common to all. … It might be that the only common feature uniting the members of such an extensive symbolic class was that they belong together, to that class. (Needham 1979, 63–4)

The members of a class may be so different that the only common trait might be that they are members of the same class. For instance, perhaps the only thing common to all "women" is that they are called "women."

There are three key arguments against essentialism that are worth mentioning here. We already have the first: categories often group together dissimilar things. We should not project essences behind labels because the things that fall behind the labels are often dissimilar.

Second, the things that fall under a classification or category change or evolve. As the famous saying goes, "you can never step in the same river twice." If one steps in the Mississippi river, steps out, and then steps back in, the river is now something different than it was the first time. Rivers are made out of water that is constantly moving, shifting, and changing. The same is true of everything in the world. It is obvious with things like "rivers" or "tornadoes," but less obvious with things like "Craig Martin." However, "Craig Martin" is constantly changing too. Not only does one's body constantly change—cells are being created and dying, digestion is taking place, oxygen is moving in and carbon dioxide moving out—but one's mind is constantly changing as well, especially as one gains new experiences, discards old ideas for new, and so on. To return to an example used above: the range of stuff that falls under the category "woman" changes as people change their use of the word, but the body of any particular "woman" is also constantly changing. As soon as we try to essentialize a "woman," perhaps by attributing to her the "ability to carry and bear a child," she may go through menopause and, in fact, no longer be able to carry or bear children. (This is, of course, leaving aside that many of those persons classed under the category of "woman" are never capable of bearing children in the first place.)

In addition, even apparently "solid" things like those that fall under the classification "tables" change: underlying the appearance of solidity are molecules and atoms constantly swirling, moving, and shifting. In addition, the wood that the table is made out of is slowly decaying. It might not decay in our lifetimes, but it will not be here in 1,000 years. Every bit of "solid" matter is shifting and moving like a river, even if it is not noticeable to a human eye. To return to another previous example: the range of stuff that falls under the category of "planet" changes as the use of the word changes, but even a particular thing falling under a specific use of that term is itself changing. Whether or not we call Pluto a "planet," the material out of which Pluto is made is shifting and changing (the changing nature of "planets" is even more obvious with gas giants such as Jupiter, which are basically clouds of swirling hydrogen and helium). Projecting an unmoving, stable essence behind our categories results in making us forget the shifting, changing nature of the stuff grouped together by those categories.

The third problem with essentialism is connected to the second. Not only are the things under our categories constantly shifting—even if slowly—but every "thing" is, in fact, a "thing" only in and through a set of relationships. The philosopher Julian Baggini tells a story that illustrates this point:

> Barbara and Wally jumped into the taxi at Oxford station. "We're in a hurry," said Barbara. "We've just done London and are heading to Stratford-upon-Avon this afternoon. So please could you show us the university and then bring us back to the station."
>
> The taxi driver smiled to himself, set the meter running and looked forward to receiving a big fare.
>
> He took them all round the city. He showed them the Ashmolean and Pitt Rivers museums, as well as the botanic gardens and the museums of natural history and the history of science. His tour took in not only the famous Bodleian library, but the lesser known Radcliffe, Sackler and Taylor libraries too. He showed them all thirty-nine colleges as well as the seven

> permanent private halls. When he finally pulled up at the station, the meter showed a fare of £64.30.
>
> "Sir, you are a fraud!" protested Wally. "You showed us the colleges, the libraries and the museums. But, damn you, we wanted to see the university!" (Baggini 2006, 145)

The same point was made even more simply by a friend of mine who once joked when passing me a bowl of ice cream: "don't worry about your diet—I personally picked out the calories by hand." The joke is that a "university" or a "calorie" is not an essence that we can find and put our finger on. The university is what we call all these buildings, the staff, the faculty, and the students *in relationship* to one another. A calorie is not a "thing," it is an energy measurement—knowing how many "calories" there are in something does not tell us what "things" are there, it tells us what sort of energy could be produced were we to burn what is there. Even a "material" thing is a set of relations; for instance, a set of relations between protons, neutrons, and electrons, or, on a more general level, relations between "table legs" and a "table top." If we take the legs off, cut apart the table top, even turn the whole thing to sawdust looking for its table-essence, we will not find it—any more than we can find a "calorie" by spooning through a bowl of ice cream. There are no essences underlying the set of relations—the "thing" *is* a set of relations grouped together under our categories.

We regularly project stable, unchanging essences where there are none—despite all these obvious problems with essentialism. Projecting a causal essence behind a group or a class is just like projecting a causal animating spirit behind rain: the rain god *causes* rain to come, and the female essence of women *causes* women to behave the way they do. Presuming that members of a group share an identical causal essence is no different than animism. Despite all of our so-called "scientific progress," we are no different than ancient communities: presuming all women share a hidden essence that determines their behavior (gender essentialism) is exactly like presuming that the rain gods are behind the rain (animism).

In addition to gender essentialism and race essentialism, we also often see religious essentialism: the idea that everyone in a particular religious group shares in some essence that determines their behavior from the inside out. Millions of people today think that there is some sort of violent essence to Islam that makes all Muslims act violently.

These people—many of whom are Christian—will point to violent passages in the Qur'an that recommend taking up arms against idolaters. The presumption seems to be that because it is in the Qur'an, it must be part of the Muslim essence, and every Muslim must therefore want to kill idolaters. The most obvious problem with this is, of course, that there are many more injunctions to kill idolaters in the Christian scriptures. There are commands to kill idolaters, commands to attack cities and kill everything that breathes, and Jesus himself is reported as saying "I came not to bring peace, but a sword." One author writing on the issue of "religious violence" even goes so far as to suggest the following: "The DNA of early Judaism, Christianity and Islam code for a lot of violence" (Hagerty 2010). The suggestion that these religions have DNA is exactly what I am talking about: the author is projecting some sort of animating essence behind the religious traditions that determines the behavior of all members of these religious traditions. However, if Islam is inherently violent because of two or three passages in the Qur'an, then Christianity is much more inherently violent because of its dozens of violent recommendations.

There is no hidden essence to any religion—violent or otherwise. If we peek behind the labels, we will find only difference, evolution, and sets of relations. Neither Islam nor Christianity are intrinsically violent, because they are not intrinsically anything. Religions do not have DNA, any more than thunder gods lie behind thunder.

3

How Society Works: Structure

Socialization and Social Order

Societies are largely constituted by systems of classification and related social roles and behavioral practices. All societies are made up of categories that distinguish between who is included and who is excluded, and, in addition, categories that distinguish different social classes or social positions *within* the group. Sometimes these classes are implicit and informal; for instance, friendship circles tend not to have rigid insider/outsider boundaries. Sometimes these things are explicit and very formal; an assistant professor of religious studies at a college has a strict set of privileges, duties, etc., unique to that position—as opposed to an "associate professor" or a full "professor"—and written down in an official contract protected under law.

For the most part, we inherit rather than create these social systems. For instance, we are born into a world in which certain expectations are placed on men and women. In North America, most of us are taught that when a man wants to marry a woman he needs to buy a diamond ring and propose to her. There is nothing natural about this—diamond rings have not always existed, and there have been societies in which a woman (or her family) does the proposing. We as individuals did not create the diamond ring practice; rather, a long time ago others created it by altering existing engagement practices. Some businesses found they could make a lot of profit by encouraging and thereby perpetuating the practice; eventually it became a tradition that most people followed. By the time I was born, it was a tradition that was almost inviolable: I did not buy a diamond ring when I proposed to my partner, and both I and my fiancée got in trouble with our families; some families might even have prohibited the marriage.

These sorts of practices are created by human beings, but then are repeated over and over, so much so that they appear to be necessary. Peter Berger writes about such social practices as if they were "tools" created by human beings. When these systems are created, they attain the same sort of reality that a tool does:

> Once produced, the tool has a being of its own that cannot be readily changed by those who employ it. Indeed, the tool (say, an agricultural implement) may even enforce the logic of its being upon its users, sometimes in a way that may not be particularly agreeable to them. For instance, a plow, though obviously a human product, is an external object not only in the sense that its users may fall over it and hurt themselves as a result, just as they may by falling over a rock or a stump or any other natural object. ... The same objectivity, however, characterizes non-material elements of culture as well. (Berger 1967, 9)

Berger is suggesting that a society might invent a cultural product like a plow, which, once created, has a reality of its own that is to some extent outside the control of humans; if we made a knife we could also cut ourselves on it. Berger goes on to say that the same thing is true of non-material things in culture, just like the engagement ring practice. While we could not physically cut ourselves on that practice in the way that we could trip and fall over a plow, we can face significant social consequences were we to violate the social practice. The first person to wear pants probably did so out of sheer preference or pragmatism; however, this has become crystallized as an inviolable social practice. For most of us, if we went to work without pants we would lose our jobs.

The same goes for many religious traditions. Many Jewish communities forbid tattoos and require men to wear yarmulkes. Amish women are required to wear dresses and bonnets. Where such social codes are strictly enforced, violation of the code can result in serious censure. According to Berger (1967, 9), "Man concocts institutions, which come to confront him as powerfully controlling and even menacing constellations." (It would be a mistake to assume that these sorts of social strictures apply only in exotic or alien communities, and that there are no equivalents in, for instance, mainstream US culture. On the contrary, I have known many people who have been censured by their family for wearing tattoos or facial piercings, and some who have been threatened with termination from their jobs for violating dress codes.)

Once these social practices are set in motion, they tend to reproduce themselves automatically. Sociologist Émile Durkheim points out,

> it is patently obvious that all education consists of a continual effort to impose upon the child ways of seeing, thinking and acting which he himself would not have arrived at spontaneously. From his earliest years we oblige him to eat, drink and sleep at regular hours, and to observe cleanliness, calm and obedience; later we force him to learn how to be mindful of others, to respect customs and conventions, and to work, etc. If this constraint in time ceases to be felt it is because it gradually gives rise to habits, to inner tendencies which render it superfluous; but they supplant the constraint only because they are derived from it. (Durkheim 1982, 53–4)

Durkheim makes a counter-intuitive claim that is almost definitely true: as children we feel our parents' control of our lives as constraining, but we eventually become so habituated to these practices that they are no longer felt as constraints. Through habituation these practices can move from being forced on us to being actively desired by us. There is no doubt that many Jewish men enjoy wearing a yarmulke, or that many Muslim women enjoy wearing a veil. The reverse is probably true as well: most Jewish women are probably perfectly happy being *denied* the freedom to wear a yarmulke, and Muslim men probably do not feel imposed upon by being prevented from wearing a veil.

Through socialization we internalize not only these sorts of practices, but also the social positions or social roles assigned to us. These positions and roles are fundamentally inter-related to the practices—one's role in the practice of engagement rituals will depend upon whether one has been assigned the identity of "male" or "female." According to Berger (1967, 14), "The roles of, for instance, husband, father or uncle are objectively defined and available as models for individual conduct." Berger notes that an individual can "put on" these roles like he or she is putting on clothes. However, he goes on to suggest that usually these roles are internalized at a much deeper level. Along with the social roles assigned to us we receive an identity that makes us what we are. "In other words, the individual is not only expected to perform as husband, father, or uncle, but to *be* a husband, a father, or an uncle" (Berger, 1967, 14). As noted in Chapter 2, we are not naturally "male" or "female": we *are made* male or female (in part) by the classifications and social conventions we inherit. But again, these identities are so deeply internalized that individuals do not feel that they are "playing" at being a male or a female; they feel that they simply *are* a man or a woman. As Durkheim rightly insists, when we internalize these identities, they go from being "outside" us to being "inside":

> collective force is not wholly external to us; it does not entirely move us from the outside. Indeed, since society can exist only in individual minds and through them, it must penetrate and become organized inside us; it becomes an integral part of our being. (Durkheim 2001, 157)

For sociologist Anthony Giddens, what is particularly important about social identities are the *rights and responsibilities* assigned to them. For him, a social position is

> a social identity that carries with it a certain range (however diffusely specified) of prerogatives and obligations that an actor who is accorded that identity … may activate or carry out: these prerogatives and obligations constitute the role-prescriptions associated with that position.
> (Giddens 1984, 84)

That is, what rights one can claim and what responsibilities one is assigned are related to the identity one's society ascribes. These rights and responsibilities do not strictly determine how a particular individual will behave, but they undeniably limit the range of possible behaviors open to her.

As we saw in the previous chapter, the assignment of an identity is often presumed to be based on an essence. We pretend to discover an essence and attach a label to it; the truth, of course, is that we attach a label and then project an essence (and, as social constructionists note, labels group together dissimilar things that lack any sort of common essence). We usually attempt to justify the sorts of right and responsibilities we assign on the basis of that essence. We project the essence of "dumbness" behind the label "blonde," and assign rights and responsibilities accordingly:

Dumbness ← Blonde → Will make mistakes → Do not give responsibility

Again, this is a silly example, but we see the same thing done throughout history with very real categories, such as "man" and "woman," or "white" and "black." It is an almost universal feature of those cultural traditions we call religions that they assign essences and categories to groups of people. For instance, ancient Hindus divided people into four classes: priests, warriors, farmers, and servants. Extremely significant rights and responsibilities were assigned to these identities on the basis of a projected essence. Similarly, ancient Israelite texts divide Israel into twelve tribes and assign specific rights and responsibilities to some of them—for instance, the male Cohanim of the Levite tribe had the duty of serving as priests. The Catholic Church makes a fundamental division between men and women—only the former are permitted to be priests and only the latter are permitted to be nuns—and the rights and responsibilities assigned to these groups are substantially different in important ways.

Most of the identities and roles we internalize are not like our career identities. Most professors could, at some point in the future, decide they did not want to be professors anymore and quit their jobs—thereby altering their professional identity. But other identities, like race, gender, and family identity, are assigned at birth and are unlikely to be changed. These identities will be almost impossible to shake, although they too are just social constructions. In past societies "white" was not a category; if one was born in the first century, one could not have been "white." North America is patrilineal, which means that family identity is through the father; if one were born in a matrilineal society, one would bear the mother's last name rather than the father. Racial and familial identities are not natural, although they are often taken as such. Even these extremely basic identities are social constructions, and if one were born in a different society one would *be* something or someone different. In summary, through the socialization process an individual internalizes

> the roles assigned to him in this context and apprehends his own identity in terms of these roles. Thus, he not only plays the role of uncle, but he *is* an uncle. *Nor, if socialization has been fairly successful, does he wish to be anything else.* (Berger 1967, 17; emphasis added)

Or, as Pierre Bourdieu puts it,

> The work of inculcation through which the … imposition of the arbitrary limit [between one social identity and another] is achieved can seek to naturalize the decisive breaks that constitute an arbitrary cultural limit—those expressed in fundamental oppositions like masculine/feminine, etc.—in the form of a *sense of limits*, which inclines some people to maintain their rank and distance and others to know their place and be happy with what they are, to be what they have to be, thus depriving them of the very sense of deprivation. (Bourdieu 1999, 123)

That is, if one is classified as "male" and has successfully internalized one's society's construction of "male" identity, one will *want to be* male, and one will *want* male things. One will want blue rather than pink clothes, will want to wear pants rather than skirts, or will want to keep short rather than long fingernails. Of course, there is nothing natural about any of these things—pink was the popular color for boys in the past—but once one has internalized one's male identity and the coordinated male practices in my society, one will want these because they are what males are supposed to want. In addition, as Bourdieu notes, one will learn to be happy with the fact that one is prohibited from wearing skirts—one will be deprived of the sense that one is being deprived of the ability to wear skirts. As noted above, once a subject identified as both "Muslim" and "male" has internalized these identities, it is unlikely that he will have any desire to wear a veil.

Social positions are often coordinated, and the social system only works in part because individuals who have internalized the system act in concert with one another (although it is clear that the system, in fact, *never* works entirely smoothly because people *never* fully internalize the dominant order of things). Members of each social position play their part in the whole, just as on the football field quarterbacks, running backs, linesmen, etc. play their part in the whole. Society only works "if the individuals who compose it are assembled and act in common" (Durkheim 2001, 313). American evangelical Christians, for instance, sometimes have a very strict coordination of separate but complimentary gendered parenting roles. They insist that because of the way their god created human beings, men have the ability to teach children certain necessary skills every child needs to learn, but which women cannot teach—and vice versa. Consequently, they sometimes vehemently oppose gay parenting on the grounds that two men (or two women) cannot teach their children *both* sets of skills the children need to know. (Evangelicals also tend to oppose single parenting for the same reason, but interestingly without the vehemence they reserve for gays and lesbians.)

When we so deeply internalize a particular social system, we tend to take it completely for granted. We rarely, if ever, question the ways in which we have been classified. Bruce Lincoln puts it this way:

> Understanding the system of ideology that operates in one's own society is made difficult by two factors: (i) one's consciousness is itself a product of that system, and (ii) the system's very success renders its operations invisible, since one is so consistently immersed in and bombarded by its products that one comes to mistake them (and the apparatus through which they are produced and disseminated) for nothing other than "nature." (Lincoln 1996, 226)

This tendency not to question the social order we have inherited and internalized is, of course, good for social stability.

> It is much better (better, that is, in terms of social stability) if [an individual] looks upon [the identities assigned to her] as part and parcel of the "nature of things." If that can be achieved, the individual who strays seriously from the socially defined programs can be considered not only a fool or a knave, but a madman. (Berger 1967, 24)

People who do not follow the expectations of the identity assigned to them are seen as extremely disruptive of the social order, and they often are. It is for this reason, for instance, that transvestites and transsexuals are so threatening to a social order oriented around a strictly binary sexual division of labor. They are, of course, not as threatening in communities—and there are many (see Nanda 2000)—that are not so strict about sexual difference. In general, roles are created and then coordinated, and when they are, people are expected to march in unison to the beat of the drum. If one person steps out of line, she may knock other people out of line and create general disorder—as many of us have seen when one person in a marching band trips and falls, creating a domino effect. Religious traditions are often extremely strict when it comes to organizing and policing gender roles so that they remain stable. It is not very often that we find an Amish woman building a house or an Amish man cooking dinner.

It is worth noting however—and I'll have more to say about this below—that social order is not necessarily intrinsically good. One significant problem with social coordination is that the system is often set up to exploit some people for the benefit of others, in which case stepping out of line might in retrospect be justified even when it throws society out of order. The sort of social order where there is a careful coordination of the social positions "slave owner" and "slave" is extremely disrupted when slaves run away, but in these sorts of cases perhaps social disorder is preferable to social order.

Naturalization as Social Constraint

Peter Berger and Thomas Luckmann rightly insist, "Social order is not part of the 'nature of things,' and it cannot be derived from the 'laws of nature.' Social order exists *only* as a product of human activity" (Berger and Luckmann 1967, 52). However, most of the time people take social constructions for granted as if they were natural things; scholars call this "reification," "naturalization," or "mystification."

> Reification is the apprehension of human phenomena as if they were things, that is, in non-human or possibly supra-human terms. Another way of saying this is that reification is the apprehension of the products of human activity *as if* they were something else than human products—such as facts of nature, results of cosmic laws, or manifestations of divine will. (Berger and Luckmann 1967, 89)

Mary Douglas argues something similar. She suggests that obviously practical social conventions are often recognized as such—we drive on the right side of the road in North America because it is a useful or convenient social code, and the fact that it is merely a convention is generally obvious to all. However, most social practices or social institutions are not like this:

> most established institutions, if challenged, are able to rest their claims to legitimacy on their fit with the nature of the universe. A convention is institutionalized when, in reply to the question, "Why do you do it like this?" although the first answer may be framed in terms of mutual convenience, in response to further questioning the final answer refers to the way the planets are fixed in the sky or the way that plants or humans or animals naturally behave. (Douglas 1986, 46–7)

When one simply assumes that one is "white" or "black," the fact that racial categories are social constructions is forgotten. We could say that the socially constructed aspect of that identity has been mystified or naturalized. One time I wore traditionally female make-up to work as an experiment (specifically, I painted my nails pink and wore lipstick). One can imagine the responses I got: "that's just wrong!"; "but you're a guy!"; and so on. When people said these things to me they were mystifying or naturalizing certain gendered practices. There's nothing natural about our society's make-up practices—there is nothing about nail polish that makes it inherently better suited for women than for men. However, when people respond to a male wearing nail polish by saying "but you're a guy!", they are talking about that particular social norm *as if it were natural*, or as if it were built into the way the universe works. Naturalization (or mystification or reification—we are using these words interchangeably here) is one of the most powerful tools for social control available. When one breaks a social code that has been naturalized, it seems as if one has broken one of the rules of the universe—it seems like defying gravity or messing with the space–time continuum.

In addition, when people say "but you're a guy!", it seems like they are making a *descriptive* statement: it is just a matter of fact that I am a "guy." However, much more than this is going on: there are obligations affiliated with the position of a "guy" that are being *prescribed*. If I wear fingernail polish and someone says "but you're a guy," they are implicitly saying, "*and guys shouldn't do that*." That is, the "matter of fact" turns out to contain a value judgment and an order to comply with a social norm. It is for this reason that Bourdieu says, "[e]very time we use a classificatory concept … we are making both a description *and a prescription*, which is not perceived as such because it is (more or less) universally accepted and goes without saying" (Bourdieu 1998, 66; emphasis added).

Berger suggests that when human identities, practices, social structures, etc. are reified, those things are given a "fictitious necessity." That is, it seems like they are necessary when, in fact, they are not. I could have been born in a society that has three sexes, instead of two—there is nothing necessary about a two-sex or two-gender system. However, when people say "but you're a guy!", they are naturalizing the two-sex system and making it seem *as if* it were necessary. We are constantly surrounded by fictitious necessities: it seems necessary that "guys" should not wear nail polish and lipstick to work. Because we take these social practices as if they were natural and necessary (as natural and necessary as gravity, for instance), we tend to keep the practices in place. It is for this reason that Bourdieu insists that individuals "tend to reproduce this [social] order without either knowing they are doing so or wanting to do so" (Bourdieu 1998, 26). We may not *want* to keep a set of arbitrary social practices going, but because we assume they are necessary we maintain the practice without thinking about it.

It might seem as if all such naturalized social norms are merely oppressive or constraining on individuals—as if society was simply about social control. However, this seriously misunderstands the incredibly positive aspects of societies. According to Anthony Giddens, social structure "is not to be equated with constraint but is always *both constraining and enabling*" (Giddens 1984, 25; emphasis added). For example, the identity of a "professor" does, of course, *constrain* professors in some ways—there are many things that it is considered "improper" (or even illegal) for professors to do—but that identity is also *enabling*. At the very least, it enables many professors to do what they love (i.e., to teach) and to earn an income at the same time. So while professors might grumble at times about their constraints—for instance, some professors chafe against the dress codes—we can nevertheless recognize that those constraints are simultaneously coordinated with a number of positive possibilities or opportunities that would not otherwise be possible.

On the other hand, however, it is clear that naturalized social orders are often set up in ways that serve the interests of some groups more than others. For instance, even after the abolition of slavery in the United States, strict racial segregation persisted for about a century (and there is good evidence that it still persists). The practice of segregation was so taken for granted that it was a fictitious necessity. If a black person went into a "white" restaurant, people might have responded by saying "but you're black!", just as people today might say "but you're a guy!" Such a statement is not merely a description, but carries with it an entire set of social *prescriptions* as well. "But you're black" meant "get out." The complete internalization of social positions and social practices can be good for social order, but it can also reproduce oppression or domination as well. Sometimes, dominated groups even willingly participate in their own oppression: there were women in nineteenth-century America who actively campaigned *against* their own right to vote (Figure 3.1). They had so successfully internalized their subordinate social role that they accepted it as natural, right, and necessary. In a sense, this was good for social order—women were kept in line, so to speak—but these women were unintentionally reproducing a social order in which they were assigned a dominated status. It is for this reason that it is useful to continually re-evaluate the social orders in which we live: whose interests are being served by the existing social order and whose are not?

In *Emerging from the Chrysalis,* Bruce Lincoln draws from anthropological accounts of societies in cultures across the world—including the Navaho in North America, the Tiyyar in India, and the Tiv in Africa—and demonstrates how rituals that initiate girls into womanhood often function to assign an identity to women that both enables and constrains them. The title refers to the central metaphor of the book: like a caterpillar that wraps itself in a cocoon or chrysalis and later emerges as a beautiful butterfly, so young girls enter rites of passage and later emerge as women. This is a perfect example of naturalization: Lincoln presents social processes (initiation rituals) as if they were natural processes (caterpillars turning into butterflies).

For Lincoln, much of what is significant is that the girls who participate in the ritual attain a divine cosmological significance for themselves. For the Tiyyar, these rituals are necessary for the young women

POLITICAL ADVERTISEMENT POLITICAL ADVERTISEMENT

VOTERS OF MASSACHUSETTS

ONE MILLION WOMEN of Voting Age in
Massachusetts

DO NOT WANT TO FIGHT MEN IN POLITICS

Less than ONE-TENTH of that number are DEMAND-
ING THE BALLOT.

STAND WITH THE MILLION!

Woman Suffrage is a WOMAN'S question. The Suffra-
gists demand that MEN shall FORCE the burden of
politics upon ALL WOMEN Without the Consent of
Ninety Per Cent.

IS THAT DEMOCRATIC? IS IT JUST?

Woman Suffrage increases taxes, injures Women, increases
Divorce. It is a Costly and Dangerous Experiment.

Woman Suffrage is part of the Feminist Movement, and is
wanted by every Socialist, every I. W. W., and every
Mormon.

DO NOT JOIN HANDS WITH THESE ENEMIES OF
THE HOME AND OF CHRISTIAN CIVILIZATION.

The men of New Jersey voted to Protect their Women from
Politics, to Maintain the Family as the Unit of the State.

WE APPEAL TO YOU TO FOLLOW THEIR EXAMPLE.
VOTE "NO" ON WOMAN SUFFRAGE next Tuesday in

Justice to Your State and to

ONE MILLION WOMEN

WOMEN'S ANTI-SUFFRAGE ASSOCIATION OF MASSACHUSETTS,
685 Boylston Street, Boston
Mrs. John Balch, President. Mrs Charles P Strong, Secretary.

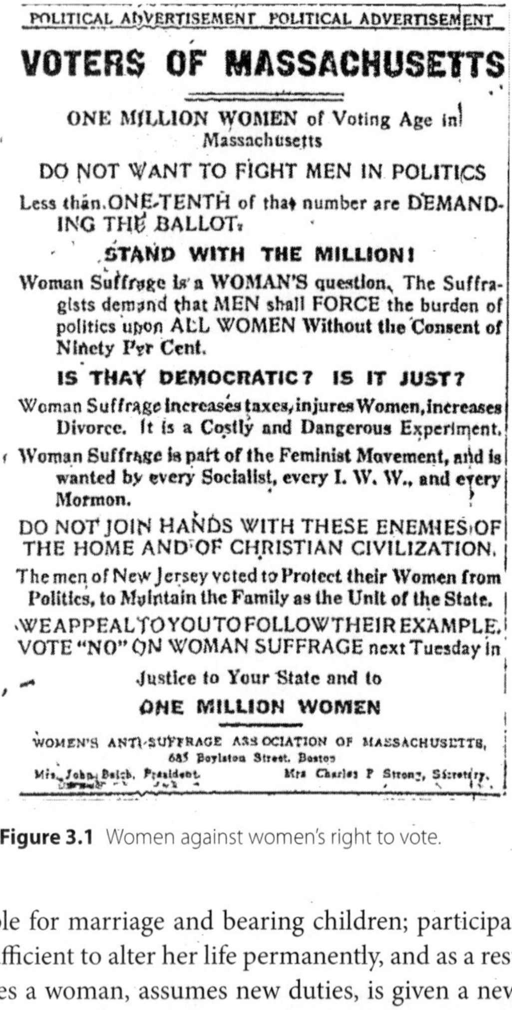

Figure 3.1 Women against women's right to vote.

to be eligible for marriage and bearing children; participation in the
ritual "is sufficient to alter her life permanently, and as a result of it the
girl becomes a woman, assumes new duties, is given a new honorific
title ... and is considered eligible for marriage" (Lincoln 1991b, 7). For
the Navajo, the ritual involves singing songs about a respected goddess
named "Changing Woman," who is associated with fertility; singing the
songs is understood to confer a symbolic identification of the young
woman with the goddess. Lincoln notes, "Social and religious factors
are not separate, but inextricably tied. Respect for Changing Woman
and respect for women in general are one and the same, for each woman
is Changing Woman, and becomes so through performance of the ...
rite" (Lincoln 1991b, 33). The Tiv ritual involves not only a symbolic
transformation brought about through song, but bodily transformation

brought about through ritual scarification. Young women who undertake the Tiv ritual have concentric circles drawn around their navel with a razor, as well as lines drawn from the navel to the throat. The scars are "said to promote fertility," and the ritual's effect

> is transformative: it is the means whereby a girl becomes a woman … The scars themselves are simultaneously the means of her transformation and the visible mark that this transformation has been completed, making each girl a woman and a sacred object for all to see. (Lincoln 1991b, 48–49)

When the first edition of his book appeared (Lincoln 1981), the text focused on the positive nature of these rituals:

> What rituals can do is to transform necessary activities from unremitting drudgery into something rich and satisfying, and filled with meaning. Ritual thus makes hunting or planting into sacred activities by defining them as repetitions of divine primordial gestures or acts necessary to preserve the cosmic order. In this way, ritual makes it possible for people to derive profound emotional and intellectual satisfaction from otherwise pedestrian affairs, because it points to something cosmic, transcendent, or sacred concealed within the tedium of mundane existence. (Lincoln 1991b, 107)

Because of such rituals, they are not just young women planting crops in the hot sun—they become goddesses making the earth fertile for the purpose of bringing life to the cosmos. The former might be boring, but the latter confers emotional satisfaction. For Lincoln, these rituals should be understood as fundamentally enabling meaning and happiness for those who undergo them.

However, ten years later Lincoln issued a second edition of *Emerging from the Chrysalis*, in which he emphasized the more oppressive side of these rituals. He wrote a new afterword, pointing out that he had changed his mind since the book first appeared. He did not deny that rituals can enable meaningful lives for women, but he noted that there is a darker side to the rituals that he had previously ignored. In part, these rituals naturalize and assign social roles these women might not otherwise have chosen. "Successful initiation … thus produces Navajo women who will put their abundant labor at the disposal of others: husbands, children, friends, relations. It produces women who serve food, keep house, tend children, till the land, herd the animals, and what is more, who learn to derive satisfaction and pride from all this" (Lincoln 1991b, 113). Lincoln suspects that this serves the interests of these women's husbands and children, for instance, more than it serves the interests of the women themselves: such rituals lead "subjects to desire (or think they desire) for themselves precisely what society desires of them" (Lincoln 1991b, 112). For Lincoln, it is almost as if these rituals make women into slaves for their societies, but slaves who have so deeply internalized their naturalized social role that they actively desire the "positions, statuses, and modes of being that society desires for and demands of them: persons it can use for its own purposes" (Lincoln 1991b, 112). In the second edition of his book, the rituals of the Navajo, Tiyyar, and the Tiv are depicted as more constraining than enabling, more exploitative than beautiful.

Elements of Societies

Given the preceding discussion, it is useful to think of societies as having the following key elements:

- insider/outsider boundaries,
- social hierarchies and social positions,
- assigned behaviors, including
  - social roles for particular positions,
  - moral codes,
  - behavioral codes,
  - etc.

These things are fairly straightforward. First, for every community there are *boundaries* designating an inside and an outside. Everyone is a member of his or her own family, but is necessarily genealogically excluded from most other families. Some insider/outsider boundaries are mutually exclusive: in the United States one cannot, technically speaking, be an official member of the Democratic Party and the Republican Party at the same time. Many religious communities see their religious identities as mutually exclusive; that is, most people believe that one cannot be, for instance, both a Christian and a Jew at the same time. This is not always the case; there are many people who consider themselves *both* Jewish *and* Christian. (And, in fact, many of the first Christians—such as Jesus' disciples—were Jews who saw the Jesus movement as just another branch of Judaism.) Most insider/outsider boundaries are obviously not mutually exclusive. One can be a member of a number of classes all at once: "female," "Catholic," "nun," "sister," "daughter," and so on—there is nothing mutually exclusive about these identities or group memberships.

As noted above, there are almost always privileges and duties associated with community membership. There will be a wide variety of social expectations, prohibitions, and privileges placed on one identified as "female," "Catholic," "nun," and so on—not the least of which is that one will be absolutely prohibited from administering certain Catholic rituals, such as the Eucharist, as that is reserved strictly for those who wear the identities "male" and "priest."

Every community has *social hierarchies*. Usually there are unique privileges and duties associated with each level of the social hierarchy. The Catholic Church has an obvious social hierarchy: there is a pope at the top, and that position is followed by a variety of bishops, priests, nuns, laypersons, etc. There is a very specific division of labor, where each level in the hierarchy is assigned a specific set of tasks. However, not all religious traditions have a formalized hierarchy. There is no Muslim or Jewish equivalent of the Catholic pope, for instance; the hierarchies in Judaism and Islam tend to be less centralized and more variable from community to community.

It should be noted that people are almost always a part of *multiple* communities or contexts at the same time. A college professor of religion could be a minister at a local church. If the college's president is a member of that church, the professor will stand above the president in the church's hierarchy but below the president in the college community. Similarly, some scholars have noted that in highly patriarchal religious communities the men may hold positions of privilege in the overall community, but as women are given charge over domestic tasks, they may have authority over men in their kitchens.

Finally, every community has certain behavioral demands or expectations for individuals in the community. College professors are obliged to dress in a manner appropriate for someone at their rank in the social hierarchy: professors need not wear a suit (as the deans or vice presidents do), but they cannot wear jeans and T-shirts like students. As noted above, if individuals have been successfully socialized—that is, if they have successfully internalized the social system—they will desire to comply with these behavior demands, rather than find them as restrictions. The same often goes for religious practitioners that are required to wear yarmulkes, bonnets, veils, and so on.

Repression and Domination

Now that we have an idea of how societies are constructed and what elements or positions exist within societies, we should consider how subjects within those positions have their interests served—or not served—by the structure of society. Any analysis of this should include, at the very least, a consideration of desires, repression, interests, and domination. The guiding question of this section is the following: how could it be possible that one could desire to enter a relationship of domination that works against one's own interests? It seems counter-intuitive: why would someone want to be dominated? After explaining repression and domination, I will demonstrate—using an anecdote from my family's history—how my grandmother's conservative Christian community socialized her into *actively desiring* to be in a dominated position within the community.

Desire and repression are rather straightforward. By "desire" we simply refer to the desires (in the colloquial sense) that subjects have—or, more precisely, *are socialized to have*—and which they express both explicitly (through what they say) and implicitly (through their behavior). Repression takes place when subjects are prevented from fulfilling their desires. Forms of repression may be superficial or severe. When a child desires to have candy for dinner and her parents prevent her from doing so, this would technically be repressive, although obviously in a minor and relatively unimportant way. By contrast, enslaving a group of people and forcing them against their will to farm one's land would be an extreme form of repression.

Interests and domination are much more complicated matters. One's interests involve not only one's immediate desires, but one's desires over time. In fact, it is important to note that repressing one's immediate *desires* may serve one's *interests* in the long run. For instance, the child that wants to eat candy for dinner every night is not aware of the fact that such behavior will damage her health and inhibit the fulfillment of her desires in the future. Consequently, repressing the child's immediate desire to eat candy for dinner will probably serve her long-term interests. For this reason it is entirely possible for one's immediate desires and one's interests to be in conflict.

While repression thwarts the satisfaction of desires, domination thwarts the satisfaction of interests. While one's desires are typically obvious—in which case repression is easy to identify—interests are more complicated and individuals often enter into relationships of domination without noticing they are doing so. It is important to distinguish between two different kinds of domination. The first is domination of a subject by another subject or group of subjects (relational domination); the second is domination of a subject's interests by a social system itself (system domination).

Relational domination

The domination of a subject in relation to other subjects in a social system can take at least three forms. First, all subjects in a social system are required to conform to social codes, many of them arbitrary. However, *subjects can be dominated when required to conform to a disproportionate number of arbitrary social codes than subjects in other positions.* Almost all social positions have some completely arbitrary social codes attached to them. Workplace dress codes are among the most obvious social codes attached to social hierarchies. At most colleges, students can wear whatever they want; faculty have to dress "more professionally" than the students; but administrators typically need to wear something much more formal. All of these social codes might serve a useful or even necessary social function of delimiting social hierarchies, but the nature of the specific codes is completely arbitrary. There is nothing about a suit that makes it intrinsically more suited to administrative work than jeans and a T-shirt. Nothing justifies the specific details of dress codes, other than the weight of tradition.

There is nothing intrinsically bad about such social codes. They make it easier for subjects to navigate social relations. As Judith Lorber notes about gendered social codes,

> Gender signs and signals are so ubiquitous that we usually fail to note them—unless they are missing or ambiguous. Then

> we are uncomfortable until we have successfully placed the other person in a gender status; otherwise we feel socially dislocated. (Lorber 1994, 14)

Seeing someone in a suit tells an individual that she can expect certain behaviors from that person; without these sorts of social markers we would be stumbling around in the dark, so to speak. Once a colleague of mine brushed off and dismissed a strange visitor to his office who stopped by to say hello, only to find out later that the visitor was a board member at the college; when he found out what he had done he was mortified. This *faux pas* would never have happened if board members wore uniforms.

Nevertheless, some arbitrary social codes are much more costly or burdensome than others. For instance, consider retail work uniforms. Some retail stores make their employees mark themselves off from customers with little more than a nametag. Others require a uniform shirt, while others require uniform hats, shirts, ties, pants, and shoes. The choice of one marker over another may not be entirely arbitrary. A security guard with a head-to-toe uniform would be more visibly obvious—and therefore more able to dissuade thieves—than a security guard with nothing more than a nametag. However, in most cases of these sorts the social markers are equally functional—one marker would be just as good as another. But some businesses choose social markers that are quite burdensome on their employees. It would typically be received as more burdensome to have to purchase a full uniform, as compared with a mere shirt or nametag. In those situations we can say that those employees are in a relationship of domination compared with those people in the social hierarchy that are not required to purchase expensive uniforms.

Of course, whether or not such requirements are received or felt as burdensome will be relative to a subject's desires. Whereas a retail employee might find purchasing a full uniform to be needlessly expensive, some people entering the business world out of college look forward to getting a well-paying job so that they can afford to purchase expensive suits to demarcate themselves from the general population. Those suits are expensive, and their selection as a social marker is arbitrary, but such subjects might in fact *enjoy* this requirement. For this reason the multiplication of arbitrary social codes is not necessarily received as burdensome or repressive in and of itself.

However, despite the fact that some individuals might have developed a desire for the arbitrary social codes placed on them, such demands would nevertheless not serve their general interests because *their desires might change*. Many young women in American society desire to comply with the requirement that they shave their legs and armpits. This is an arbitrary and unnatural social requirement for conformity to the North American ideal or norm of femininity; however, many young women are so socialized into North American bodily practices that *not* to shave would make them feel extremely uncomfortable. The socialization process has directed their desires toward that social practice. Shaving makes them feel good about themselves. However, some young women experience a change in their desires. Whereas they once desired to shave, they no longer have such a desire. Nevertheless, our society *still places that demand for conformity* on subjects in the social position of "female." (It is not, of course, a legal requirement, but women who choose to violate this arbitrary social code may lose much of their social privilege or social capital or find themselves suffering from discrimination in a number of implicit and explicit ways—a woman who refuses to shave her legs has little chance of being hired as a waitress or flight attendant where skirts are part of the uniform.) When these women's desires change, they find the demand to comply with the arbitrary social code to be considerably burdensome. To reiterate the main point here: this requirement that women shave their legs may not be repressive if a woman desires to do so, but the requirement may work against her long-term interests because her desires may change. It is for this reason that it serves one's long-term interests to have *fewer* arbitrary social codes demanded for successful conformity to one's social position. By contrast, it puts women in a relationship of domination to men to have a disproportionate number of arbitrary social codes placed on them compared with men.

Interestingly, in many religious communities a greater number of arbitrary social codes may be required of elites than laity. The pope is required to wear a very specific uniform, whereas lay members of the Catholic Church have a great deal of freedom concerning what they may wear to mass. In this way the pope is—to a small degree—dominated.

A second form of relational domination involves asymmetrical access to capital, privilege, and authority, as well as the means to manipulate, produce, or reproduce these. By capital we mean all of the following: material capital (such as money, property, etc.), cultural capital (knowledge or mastery of cultural elements that garner respect in a particular society—for instance, the ability to quote Shakespeare means more in predominately white societies than does the ability to quote Tupac Shakur), and social capital (network connections to and respect of peers or superiors with their own capital, privilege, or authority). By privilege we refer to advantages or benefits conferred on a subject—but denied to others—simply because of his or her social position. By authority we refer to the ability to direct the behavior of others without the use of force. Obviously these elements are not mutually exclusive and overlap to some extent (for instance, authority typically operates in ways related to cultural capital and social capital); they are not intended to be understood as discreet and unrelated. I take it for granted that it is obvious how access to capital, privilege, and authority serves one's interests. Subjects with capital, privilege, and authority are much more capable of satisfying their interests.

Consequently, *a subject is dominated when those in her social position have a disproportionate access to these when compared with subjects in other social positions*. Studies have shown, for instance, that women systematically make less money than men in the same jobs; we could therefore say that in this matter women are dominated. In most religious communities elites have much greater privilege and authority than the laity. Although the pope is perhaps slightly dominated by the greater number of restrictions placed on his dress, he is obviously in a substantial position of domination when it comes to access to privilege and authority.

Third, it serves one's interests to be able to alter the social arrangements in which one is situated. This includes the ability to move subjects (either oneself or others) from one social position to another social position *or* to rearrange the relationship between social positions. The ability to move subjects from position to position would include the ability to promote or demote subjects in a social hierarchy. For instance, college presidents generally have the power to fire untenured professors, but that power is not reciprocal, of course. In addition, the ability to rearrange the relationship between social positions would be something like the ability to change a social hierarchy. For instance, many college presidents have the power not only to hire or fire people into or from existing positions, but to create and eliminate positions in the hierarchy altogether.

The reason this ability serves a subject's interests is because when the social arrangements are not well suited to work toward the satisfaction of an individual's desires, she can change the social arrangements so that they will. Consequently, *domination takes place when subjects in particular positions have a disproportionate ability to alter those arrangements, compared with subjects in other social positions.* In patriarchal religious communities, for instance, it is usually the case that the patriarch can make decisions that will alter the family's social arrangements (for instance, the patriarch might be able to decide to move the family to another country) in ways that other members of the family cannot.

In college classrooms, those in the social position of "professor" have more of an ability to alter the social arrangements than do those in the position of "student." Theoretically, this relationship of domination is justified: professors are supposed to have a pedagogical expertise that justifies the fact that the professor writes the syllabus rather than the students. In addition, the professor is ideally serving the interests of the students in other ways by providing them with knowledge, skills, or credentials that will facilitate the students' future ability to fulfill their desires. However, it is not at all clear that these justifications work. Some would argue that the requirement of a college degree as a condition for some positions in society is actually arbitrary—a college degree may be no more intrinsically necessary for a position in society than wearing nail polish is intrinsically necessary for women. If the requirement of this degree is, in fact, arbitrary, then professors are not only in a relationship of domination with their students—as they have more power to alter the social arrangements—but also a relationship of *exploitative* domination—as professors clearly benefit from the general requirement of a college degree (that is, professors make a salary that students indirectly pay for in pursuit of the degree). In the United States, for example, it is increasingly expected that just about everyone should go to college, and professors indirectly benefit from that general expectation.

System domination

One can also be dominated by a social system when the system creates subjects with tragic interests, where tragic interests are defined as ones that cannot be served by the system. Here is a somewhat silly example of an extremely common yet mild form of domination: North American culture creates a large number of subjects who desire to be famous: movie stars, rock stars, etc. However, the way the culture is set up makes it impossible for every subject who desires to be a rock star to be one. The widespread interest in being a rock star is a tragic interest—it is impossible for all of those interests produced by the system to be satisfied by the system.

Judith Lorber notes, in *Paradoxes of Gender*, that males and females are socialized in contemporary Western societies in ways that are paradoxical.

> [F]emininity is framed by a relationship with one man that is romantic at first and sexual later, but masculinity is framed by sexual conquests of many women and only secondarily by an emotional attachment to one. To be considered feminine, a woman has to pry a man loose from his friends and cleave him to her; sex is her lure. To prove he is masculine, a man has to show his friends that he is a sexual conqueror; an emotional attachment to one woman can feel like a trap.
>
> (Lorber 1994, 69)

As far as this is correct—to some extent it is a generalization, and there are exceptions—we could say that this is an example of tragic interests: heterosexual men and women are socialized into their gender roles in such a way as to permit neither group to satisfy their interests fully. In such a case we could say that the system of gender roles dominates subjects in that system.

Here is perhaps a more serious example: North American culture produces a great many subjects whose long-term interests involve the hope for a highly romanticized "American dream"—a perfect heterosexual marriage, 2.4 children, a house with a two-car garage and a white picket fence, etc. Unfortunately, these are tragic interests; the capitalist economy, in its current incarnation, will not permit all who desire this ideal to participate in it. In particular, through no fault of their own, many baby boomers to whom this ideal was promised have seen their livelihood or retirement plans destroyed with the downturn in the American economy—as a result of events which were completely outside of their control. These individuals have interests that will not be able to be served by the United States' economic system. In these cases, then, we can say that they are *dominated* by the system that produces tragic interests in them.

What primarily distinguishes system domination from relational domination is that for the latter one group of subjects can benefit at the expense of others' domination, but when it comes to system domination everyone might lose by the social arrangements.

The concept of domination is most useful where domination typically remains invisible. For instance, few people today would be interested in trying to justify the obviously disproportionate number of arbitrary social norms placed on women's bodies; merely drawing attention to the fact that a relationship of domination exists can be damning.

To return to our opening question: how is it possible that someone could actively desire to enter a relationship in which he or she is dominated? As we have defined these terms, it would be nonsensical to say one desires one's own repression, but desiring domination is an entirely different matter. It should be clear by now that almost all positions are in some way subjected to domination in relation to other positions, and as such it is actually hard to imagine a set of relationships entirely free of domination. If one desires to fit into *any* position in society, then it is likely that one desires a relationship of subordination.

However, some people even desire to submit themselves to relations of domination that are quite substantial. Sometimes people willingly enter substantial relationships of domination because the alternative is worse: women in abusive patriarchal relationships often stay with their boyfriends or husbands simply because the alternative is to be homeless. Every year people take bad jobs—jobs where they are exploited by the company they work for—simply because the alternative is to have no job at all. Some social theorists might say that because those sorts of jobs are willingly taken, no ethical norms are violated by the domination that results. However, if this principle stands—that is, if a relationship of domination is always morally acceptable when willingly entered—then it follows that it is morally acceptable for heterosexual men to beat their wives if their wives willingly "choose" to stay, even if the wives only stay because being beaten is better than being homeless. I take this to be an absurdity, and it is for this reason that I absolutely reject the idea that a relationship of domination willingly entered is intrinsically acceptable.

A second reason why one might enter a substantial relationship of domination is because one *actively* desires it. As I noted above, there were women in the nineteenth century who actively campaigned against their own right to vote. It is unlikely that these women were forced to tour the country campaigning against their own rights out of a desire to avoid a worse situation; on the contrary, they *actively desired* a subordinate position (in relationship to men) in American politics. This is perhaps the most insidious form of domination—when subjects are socialized not only to accept it but to desire it. When social systems repress our desires it is usually obvious to us; when they produce a desire for subordination—and when that desire is fulfilled—we are unlikely to notice that we are dominated.

One of the most heartbreaking examples of a relationship of domination willingly entered concerns my grandmother. She grew up in a conservative Christian community wherein women—but not men—were prohibited from wearing pants. They interpreted the Bible as prohibiting cross-dressing of any sort, and they saw pants as a "male" clothing item. This would count as a relationship of domination because this was one of a large number of completely arbitrary social norms disproportionately required of women in her community. However, my grandmother fully internalized the social norms, and therefore desired to always wear skirts and dresses, and looked askance at those women who did wear pants. To my knowledge this relationship of domination was willingly entered, and therefore in no way was she repressed.

Late in life, however, she experienced a stroke that seriously debilitated one side of her body. It became much harder for her to take care of herself, get dressed, and so on. In addition, since she could not entirely control her body, when she wore skirts or dresses it become more likely that she would sit down or fall down in ways that her underwear would show, producing some shameful or embarrassing situations. Because of this her *desires* began to change. She no longer was entirely opposed to wearing pants; in fact, she actually started wearing sweat pants, both because they covered her well and because they were easier to slip on and off than other types of clothing.

Her experience and consequent change in desire did not alter the community's expectations. As far as they were concerned, a rule was a rule—there was nothing in the Bible about permitting cross-dressing in the case of a stroke. They stuck to their arbitrary social norm. As a result, my grandmother was shamed by her peers into going back to wearing skirts and dresses, despite the increased difficulty these gave her.

This case is perhaps a paradigmatic example of the necessity for a distinction between repression and domination. My grandmother, prior to her stroke, was not repressed by this arbitrary social norm—she actively desired to wear the clothes her community desired for her. However, she was nevertheless in a relationship of domination. The arbitrary social norm did not repress her immediate desires, but since her *interests* included desires that can (and did) change over time, the arbitrary social norm she actively desired to follow nevertheless worked against her long-term interests.

We are surrounded by social structures with which subjects actively desire to comply. On the one hand, we can ask if these social structures serve the *desires* of subjects in the system; on the other hand, we can ask if these social structures serve the *interests* of subjects in the system. We should not, however, confuse these two radically different questions.

4

How Society Works: Habitus

Most of the key concepts discussed in this book—such as socialization, domination, legitimation, authority—are broadly used by scholars. Almost all social theorists, sociologists, and cultural anthropologists for the last two hundred years have utilized these concepts in one way or another; they are common fare. By contrast, the concept of *habitus* is much less broadly utilized. (Note: the plural of habitus is habitus; readers must determine whether the word is singular or plural from context.) This concept can be found here and there in western philosophy and social theory, and anthropologist Marcel Mauss reintroduced it in the early twentieth century, but it was importantly picked up and significantly revised by sociologist Pierre Bourdieu and his disciples in the second half of the twentieth century. He revised this concept in order to address what he saw as some of the weaknesses of traditional sociological accounts of how social order is reproduced over time. It should be clear that the root of habitus is "habit," and the concept does indeed concern human habits. One's habitus is the result of socialization, and is related to the fact that one develops habits linked to one's social class. For Bourdieu, these habits work—independently of an individual's conscious intentions—to reinforce social hierarchies. At the end of this chapter we will see how it is possible for a religious community to have its own unique habitus, and how this has the effect of reinforcing group boundaries.

To understand the concept of habitus and to situate it in the context of Bourdieu's thought, it will be necessary to back up and explain what Bourdieu was using the concept in part to criticize. So before we get to a full explanation of what Bourdieu means by habitus, we will need to consider what he was fighting against: the concept of *meritocracy.*

Meritocracy

By definition, a meritocracy is a society in which people get what they earn, deserve, or *merit*. Usually a meritocracy is contrasted with a type of society in which rights and privileges are assigned by birth, rather than by merit. This oversimplifies things quite a bit, but in medieval Europe there were primarily three social classes: royalty (kings, queens, etc.), nobility (lords, ladies, etc.), and serfs. In this system each class had radically different rights and privileges, and the classes were in a relationship of exploitative domination: for the most part, the royalty and nobility lived off of the work of the serfs. In addition, one's class was assigned at birth, and social mobility—specifically *upward* mobility—was denied. If one was born a serf, one would remain a serf for life—there was absolutely no way to become royalty, no matter how hard one tried.

By contrast, or so the story goes, in a meritocracy one can be born poor, but if one works hard enough one can work one's way up to an elite level. Talk of meritocracy is usually linked to "rags-to-riches" stories: one can be born "dirt poor" but die a billionaire, if only one works hard enough. Alongside rags-to-riches stories is talk of personal responsibility: if one is not doing well in life, it is probably the result of one's own (lack of) effort, for which only oneself is personally responsible. In a meritocracy, one's social class (and the privileges that come with class) are determined not by birth but by one's merit and hard work. In principle, meritocracy allows for a great deal of upward (and downward) mobility.

Consider the American myth: although the United States began as a class-based society where race predetermined one's social status, those class assignments based on race have since been outlawed, and today African-Americans have risen to the highest classes in American society—the country even has a black president. Although it began as a society in which class was based in part on race, today it has become a society in which class is based on merit. Anyone can become a millionaire or a president, if only one works hard enough.

So we have a distinction here between two types of society: one where class and privilege are assigned at birth, and one where class and privilege are based on merit and hard work. The problem, for a social theorist like Bourdieu, is that *meritocracy is a myth*. The American myth that alleges racism is over and anyone can get ahead if only they work hard enough is told without any attention whatsoever to the fact that wealth and income gaps between whites and blacks in America have actually *grown* rather than lessened in the last few decades, which is a serious problem for this myth (see Lui 2006)—and Bourdieu can offer a reasonable explanation of what this myth ignores.

We do not, in fact, live in a meritocracy, and never have. Although individuals are not locked into a class on the basis of birth, Bourdieu would argue that we are largely—although not entirely—locked into class on the basis of our habitus.

Habitus

Bourdieu defines habitus as follows:

> The conditionings associated with a particular class of conditions of existence produce *habitus*, systems of durable, transposable dispositions, structured structures predisposed to function as structuring structures, that is, as principles which generate and organize practices and representations that can be objectively adapted to their outcomes without presupposing conscious aiming at ends or an express mastery of the operations necessary in order to attain them. (Bourdieu 1990, 53)

The discussion that follows is based in part on the same text as the above definition is from, as well as his *Practical Reason* (1998) and *Language and Symbolic Power* (1999), but most of all on his book on class distinction (Bourdieu 1984).

Bourdieu's definition—and his writing style in general—is notoriously opaque, but the basic elements are not too difficult to understand. First, when Bourdieu mentions "structured structures" and "structuring structures," he is suggesting something like the following (which we covered in a different way in Chapters 2 and 3). Our society (a structure) is built out of (or structured by) the classifications we use;

our classifications constitute the blueprint we use to build our world. In addition, subjects internalize, through the process of socialization, those classifications—as well as the coordinated practices of rights and responsibilities—we see in the world once it has been built. Sometimes Bourdieu calls the set of classifications our "matrix of perception," by which he means the matrix of classifications through which we perceive the world. In summary, we build a world with our classifications; we view the world built through our matrix of perception; and in turn we ourselves are structured by those classifications, and the rights and responsibilities connected to each. *We build the world, but then it builds us.* It is important, however, to note that according to Bourdieu the set of classifications one uses, or one's matrix of perception, varies from class to class, even within the same society.

Second, what is important are *dispositions*. For Bourdieu, we all have dispositions socialized into us at a young age, and our habitus is that part of our selves where our dispositions lie. Bourdieu says that these dispositions also are produced by a particular class of conditions; what he means here is that we are all socialized in different ways depending on the society or class in which we were born. At the very least, then, we can clarify the definition of habitus in the following way: *habitus is that part of oneself where one's matrix of perception lies and where one's dispositions (or predispositions) sit, and all of this is the result of a process of socialization that varies by one's society and class.*

We can draw examples from our predispositions about what is disgusting. We tend to have "gut reactions" when we see someone eating something that disgusts us. However, what is particularly significant about those gut reactions is that they vary from place to place. Foods that are a "delicacy" elsewhere might be "disgusting" here. In some societies, animals like fish and fowl are presented at the dinner table with the head intact. Because of how socialization takes place in those societies, that is "normal," although in the United States that is usually considered "disgusting." Consider caviar: even in the US, the response to caviar depends on one's social class. Those who grow up in blue-collar families are much more likely to respond to caviar with disgust ("Fish eggs? Sick!") than those who grow up in elite, wealthy families ("Caviar? Delicious!"). One's habitus in this case is linked not only to one's society in general, but also to one's particular class.

Dispositions is a rather broad term, and there are many things that Bourdieu would include under the term. Dispositions include:

- preferences or tastes,
- abilities to distinguish between subtle differences,
- ideas of success or life goals, and
- one's *practical sense.*

Preferences or tastes are fairly straightforward: what one prefers, likes, or dislikes depends in part on one's socialization into a particular class.

One key reason why tastes are linked to class is because people tend "to make a virtue out of necessity," as the saying goes. What the saying means is that people can see what they are forced to do as a result of their life circumstances as if it were both something they chose or desired and something virtuous. People who cannot afford "nice" cars might say to themselves: "all I want is a vehicle to get me from point A to point B—having an expensive car is a needless luxury." In doing so they are "making a virtue out of necessity" by taking what they cannot do and thinking of it both as something they don't want to do and as something that would be possibly immoral to do.

We tend to think of taste as an extremely personal thing, but Bourdieu's research shows that it is not. The tastes of members of the working class do not vary greatly—rarely do they have expensive tastes. There is always some individual variation of course, but for the most part members of a class commonly share the same tastes. If tastes are the result of "making a virtue out of necessity," this is exactly what we would expect—at least when it comes to poorer classes—and that is precisely what Bourdieu's research finds. If someone is a "meat and potatoes" eater, that may not be "personal" so much as class-based—it might mean she grew up in a family that "preferred" those simple foods merely because that was all they could afford.

The ability to distinguish between subtle differences is more complicated. The basic idea is that there are innumerable differences between things in the world, and what differences we are able to notice or draw attention to will depend on how we have been socialized. For instance, my father grew up in a blue-collar family, and classic American sports cars were important to him. Consequently, I was raised capable of telling the difference between 1967, 1968, and 1969 Chevrolet Camaros. These cars are different in lots of ways: colors, wheels, stripes, bumpers, etc. Which things are essential for determining which is a '67, which is a '68, and which is a '69? I know that Figure 4.1 depicts a '67 because it lacks turn signal lights on the side of the car; Figure 4.2 depicats a '68 because it *does* have the turn signal lights on the side; and Figure 4.3 depicts a '69 because it has a crease along the side of the body, which starts just above the wheel well. This ability to differentiate the subtle differences between these three cars is part of my class habitus. Those socialized in classes different from my own may not be able to spot these differences.

Figure 4.1 Chevrolet Camaro, 1967 (Creative Commons Copyright (cc) Nathan Bittinger).

Figure 4.2 Chevrolet Camaro, 1968 (Creative Commons Copyright (cc) Rex Gray).

Although my father grew up in a blue-collar family, he was sufficiently upwardly mobile that I grew up more or less in a middle-class home. As a middle-class white male who pursued a PhD, I developed a taste for expensive beers and "microbrews," which is relatively common for people with my social background and income level. I could do a blind taste test and tell the difference between a lager, an ale, a porter, and a stout. To someone who doesn't drink expensive beer, however, the subtle differences (or not so subtle, actually, to my palette), will not be detectable. By contrast, I cannot tell the difference between a merlot, a shiraz, a cabernet sauvignon, and a zinfandel, but for those born into a wealthier class than I, the differences might be easier to spot. While a theorist like Bourdieu would not insist that the ability to distinguish subtle differences is always linked to class (many are linked to age difference, it seems), those abilities are *often* linked to class.

Ideas of success and life goals are also part of one's habitus. Growing up in an upwardly mobile family and having a father with a college education, I was taught (actually, it was merely assumed) that someday I would go to college—a college education was taken for granted as normal for someone in my social class. By contrast, I have extended family members who see going to college as undesirable or unlikely. I have a young cousin who does not have role models with a college

Figure 4.3 Chevrolet Camaro, 1969 (Creative Commons Copyright (cc) RussBowling).

education, and as such she is not sure she will be able to get into college, afford college, or complete college. Whereas it was merely taken for granted for my family, in her family it is on the outskirts of what is possible. For Bourdieu, life goals may also be the result of "making a virtue out of necessity": people who are unlikely to be able to afford to go to college may internalize their life possibilities and, as a result, view college as unnecessary and undesirable. Consequently, the reason why they may not go to college may have nothing to do with their intellectual ability, but everything to do with the internalization of expectations for members of their class.

> If French working-class youth did not appear to aspire to high levels of education attainment during the rapid educational expansion of the 1960s—and according to Bourdieu they did not—this was because they had internalized and resigned themselves to the limited opportunities that previously existed for their success in school. (Swartz 1997, 104)

Bourdieu sometimes talks about this using the phrase "the hysteresis effect," a term he appropriated from the hard sciences. It refers to an effect where elements in a system are slow to respond to changes in the system. For Bourdieu, we sometimes see the hysteresis effect in families with upward mobility: with new means they can afford to aspire to new life goals, but they tend to fall back on the life goals to which they were previously adjusted.

Practical sense is a broad term, and refers loosely to the practical ability to interact "appropriately" with others on an everyday basis. When we meet someone new and that person reaches out her hand and places it mid-air in front of us, we know exactly what to do: stretch out an arm, hold her hand in ours, and gently shake. There is nothing universal about a handshake, but because we are socialized from birth in our society to know how to respond to one, that action becomes a part of our practical sense. It is something that is second nature, and we do it without reflection and without thinking. Having a practical sense is like having a skill in sports. In the United States, children are taught how to play baseball, and this involves knowing how to hold a baseball bat, for instance. If one is right-handed, one must place the right hand above the left, at a certain spot near the base of the bat, and one is supposed to grip it tightly (but not too tightly). Over time, this ability becomes internalized as a part of one's practical sense. We do not have to consciously think about it if we pick up a bat—we grab it and naturally put our hands in the right spot. The concept of practical sense can be broken down to include at least the following:

- language, diction, or ways of speaking,
- ways of carrying one's body, or other bodily habits, and
- one's idea of what counts as "reasonable" or "common sense."

Language, diction, and ways of speaking would involve, for instance, things like accent, slang, or the ability to speak "proper" language in "proper" settings. One might hear the slang word "slut" from an individual with one habitus, but for an alternative habitus one might hear the phrase "flagrantly accessible woman." Those with a blue-collar habitus are more likely to speak loudly or boisterously, while those from wealthy classes are more likely to speak softly and with reserve. In the American south, people tend to use the word "ya'll" (a contraction of "you all") for the plural form of "you," but in the American Midwest people tend to use "you guys" for the same thing. This last example is a regional distinction rather than a class-based one, but the point is the same: how one speaks will depend on how one's habitus is socialized to speak.

Ways of carrying one's body and other bodily habits are also socialized into one's habitus. Just as blue-collar people will tend to speak more loudly than wealthy people, so wealthy people will tend to be more reserved with their body movements than blue-collar people. Wealthy people are unlikely to gesticulate wildly, or to high-five one another with energy, or have other sorts of fancy handshakes—all of which might be common for men in a blue-collar workplace. A similar notable point is that people from different regions and social classes will have different ideas about what counts as "personal space." Some people will tend to stand closer while talking and others will stand further apart—and these differences will often line up with class or regional differences.

The third part of one's practical sense includes one's idea of what counts as reasonable or common sense. In actuality, "common sense" is an oxymoron: what people take to be common sense varies from region to region and from class to class, in which case there is nothing "common" about it. What professors take to be common sense or reasonable will probably be rather different from what students take to be common sense (in fact, professors regularly lament their students' lack of common sense). One important consequence of this is that if two people are from different classes, they may both have common sense according to their own class, but may see the other person as lacking common sense—simply because their standards for what is commonsensical or reasonable are different from one another.

Because they are so clearly linked up with social classes, habitus—and their individual elements—can be markers of social boundaries. People like cheap beer not only because they are "making a virtue out of necessity"—they like it in part because it is a point of pride for members of their social group. Ordering a "Bud Light" at a bar can be like running up a flag—it sends a signal to other patrons that one is a member of a particular group—and groups are usually proud of their flags. "We're not spoiled rich pansies—we like *real* beer," or so they might say. I personally don't like cheap beer; I prefer expensive "microbrews." It is no surprise that this preference is extremely similar to other people in my social class. By drinking Smuttynose Old Brown Dog Ale I can distinguish myself from the "hoi polloi," who drink beers like Bud or Coors Light. If we looked for some objective qualities that make one beer objectively better or worse than another, we would be out of luck. A preference for *any* sort of beer is usually an acquired taste—an "objective" third party who had never had any beer would probably like neither choice. Why do we acquire tastes the way we do? Probably as a result of our class location. In summary, tastes both "make a virtue out of necessity" and serve as social boundary markers.

Of course, few people consciously reflect on their habitus, how it works, or how they got the tastes or ideas of common sense they have inherited. On the contrary, habitus is something that is thoroughly naturalized and taken for granted—it usually operates without people thinking about it. In part, this is what Bourdieu is talking about when he says that part of one's habitus is the ability to act "without presupposing conscious aiming at ends or an express mastery of the operations necessary in order to attain them." One's practical sense is internalized just as playing a sport is internalized: good athletes do not consciously think "when the ball comes I need to move my two arms in unison so that the bat strikes the ball at an ideal location." In fact, if an athlete consciously thought about her actions this way, it would probably ruin her athleticism. She might not even be able to explain explicitly what she does to others. "You can't learn how to swim without jumping in the water," as the saying goes: it is something your body learns, not something your mind consciously comprehends.

So when Bourdieu says that one acts "without presupposing conscious aiming at ends or an express mastery of the operations necessary in order to attain them," he means that because of how habitus works people usually act in the world, often achieving their practical ends or goals, without actually thinking about what they are doing or what they want to accomplish.

Normalization, Discrimination, and Privilege

Much like so-called "common sense," what is taken to be "normal" (or a normal habitus) varies from community to community and from society to society—in which case these things are *not*, in fact, "common" or universally "normal." Even within the same society, different subgroups have variable ideas about what is "normal." What we have are societies where there are dominant and subordinate groups, and where each subgroup has its own idea of what is normal.

Usually the dominant group attempts to pass off its idea of what is normal as if it were normal universally. That is, they don't think, "this is what *we* think is normal"; they think, "this is simply what *is* normal." However, because they are the dominant group, they usually have some means of power at their disposal to enforce their idea of normalcy on others. Bourdieu suggests that there is an implicit *collusion* between members of a class—they work together or collude without intentionally doing so. Most middle-aged, white, middle-class Americans think facial piercings and visible tattoos are abnormal, while some subgroups think that facial piercings and tattoos are banal or commonplace. However, because middle-aged, white, middle-class Americans are the dominant group in many cities in the country, those individuals with facial piercings or visible tattoos might be discriminated against, especially when it comes to finding work. People with my parent's habitus, for instance, would probably discriminate against job applicants with facial piercings when conducting job interviews, simply because they would find such things to be abnormal, "weird," or "unprofessional"—all the while ignoring the fact that such things are weird or unprofessional to *themselves and the dominant group*, not to everyone.

In every society there are various groups with different habitus, each different from the others, but the dominant group lifts its own habitus up to the status of "normal," forgets that it is just one habitus alongside others, and unconsciously colludes to put in place regimes of privilege and practices of discrimination. Those in the dominant group, because they are dominant, usually have the power to exclude people with an alternate habitus from their social networks, circles of friends, and places of work. Very serious consequences can result from having a habitus different from the dominant one. Again, what is "normal" is not universally normal, but only what the dominant group takes to be normal—and which they can impose on other groups. This does not, of course, mean that in every society there is one clear dominant group and a number of obviously subordinated groups. Inter-relations in society are much more complex than that. Middle-aged, white, middle-class Americans are more or less clearly dominant in the Midwest, but much less so in New York City or Los Angeles. Facial piercings and tattoos probably do not stand out nearly as much in those cities as in conservative cities such as Indianapolis. In addition, even in cities like Indianapolis, there are probably pockets of the city where there are concentrations of people with a habitus different from the dominant one, and they may be able to impose as "normal" their own habitus *in those pockets* of the city. A Hasidic Jew would stand out in Indianapolis, but not in New York City, and there are pockets of New York City where Hasidism is dominant.

The privilege and discrimination that result from having a habitus different from the dominant one can clearly be seen in Woody Allen's film *Small Time Crooks*, which, although fictional, presents a fairly realistic portrait of what happens when different habitus intersect. In the film, Woody Allen's character, Ray, launches a bank robbery scheme with some of his peers. They rent a shop next door to a bank and set about digging a tunnel from the basement of the shop into the basement vault of the bank. Ray's wife, Frenchy (played by Tracey Ullman), opens a cookie store in the shop in order to cover up the comings and goings of the characters drilling in the basement. Their attempt to dig into the vault turns out to be a dramatic failure, but Frenchy's cookie store becomes a hit. The success of the cookie store is so great that the group starts a number of franchises, and the robbers become millionaires practically overnight. The most humorous parts of the film take place when this group of blue-collar thieves starts mixing and mingling with their new peers: the upper crust of New York City. They have radically different habitus, and stick out like a sore thumb among the wealthy class they are now a part of. Frenchy wants to acclimate to the new group, but feels so out of place that she hires a wealthy man named David (played by Hugh Grant), to give her lessons on how to behave "properly" around her wealthy new friends.

There is a scene in which Ray and Frenchy are getting ready for, and then throw, a party for their new peers, in which the differences in habitus are particularly clear. The party is being hosted in their new, upscale New York apartment, furnished with the best things their new money could buy. Of course, what counts as "best" to Ray and Frenchy, with their blue-collar habitus, is rather different than what counts as "best" to the people coming to the party.

Frenchy and Ray's idea of good food can be contrasted with the wealthy people at the party. To begin with, Frenchy wants to have what she perceives to be fancy foods. She has a strong desire to conform or acclimate to the habitus of her new peers, but because she doesn't have a wealthy habitus, she doesn't understand wealthy tastes quite correctly. She insists that the truffle shavings be thick (rather than fine, as the cook assures her they are supposed to be); she calls the escargots "snails;" and she pronounces the word crudités as crude-ites (rather than crue-de-tay). In addition, she insists that the table have "finger bowls" for finger washing at the table, despite the fact that her new cook strongly insists otherwise. By contrast, Ray—who doesn't care to conform to his new peers' habitus—thinks the menu for their party is disgusting. He makes a plea for cheeseburgers or spaghetti and meatballs, and refuses to try the escargot: "a snail leaves a little trail of scum in the yard when it walks" ("Not in France, they don't," his wife replies). Her husband accuses her: "You're so hoity-toity all of a sudden." At the party one of the guests asks for some Evian or Perrier brand water; Ray says they have anything she wants, but goes on to say that he prefers tap water himself, "because the fluoride keeps your teeth from rotting."

The tastes in clothing and décor are radically different. The black suit Ray wears to the party has some sort of gold and black band around the collar, and Frenchy wears what the guests take to be a gaudy and absurdly shiny silver dress.

The difference in practical sense stands out by the bodily and verbal interaction between Ray and his guests. Although the new butler is at the door to greet guests, when the doorbell rings Ray runs up, practically elbows the butler aside, and greets the guests himself. Rather than greeting guests formally, as they expect, Ray says "how ya doin'?" and calls one woman "honey" and another "toots." At one point Frenchy addresses the other women at the party by informally calling them "girls." Perhaps the funniest moment of the party scene is when Ray starts telling jokes to the guests. "So guy says to 'im, ya know, what do ya do for a living? He says, 'I'm a mom-back.' What's a mom-back? He says, "Ya know, I stand behind the truck—I say [waiving both arms back] mom-back, mom-back" (that is, "come on back"—his job is to wave trucks onto loading docks). The woman he's talking to doesn't laugh, and Ray tries to explain it to her again, but she still doesn't laugh. The other guests in the circle awkwardly smile at him, and Ray says "I think it was too fast for her." When the woman he's talking to doesn't get his second joke, he gives her a light backhanded slap to the shoulder.

What do the wealthy people at the party think of Frenchy and Ray's behavior? When they are out of the room, the guests converse: "I can't believe this room. This takes bad taste to new heights." "This is excruciating." "Can you believe the two of them? I can't keep a straight face." "And what she's done with this apartment: the sheer flawless vulgarity of it all." "She's the definition of bad taste." There is no conspiracy here, but this is obviously collusion.

We have here a clash of habitus. The blue-collar habitus of Frenchy and Ray could hardly be any more different from their new wealthy peers. This is the hysteresis effect in action: their habitus reflects previous socio-economic conditions, and it is extremely slow to adapt to new socio-economic conditions. We see a difference in preferences and tastes, the ability to distinguish between subtle differences, ideas related to life goals, language and diction, ways of carrying one's body (at no point do the guests at the party touch anyone other than to formally shake hands, while Ray is touching people all the time), and, ultimately, ideas of reasonableness or common sense. Because these two groups share a different habitus, the guests at the party seem to think Frenchy and Ray lack all common sense (which manifests itself to them as bad taste). Ray, by contrast, thinks *they* lack common sense (who wants to eat slimy snails?). The truth, of course, is that they have different senses, each taking their own to be "common."

Habitus and the Maintenance of Class in a "Meritocracy"

The problem, of course, is that when it comes to wealthy circles in New York City, one habitus is dominant over others. Ray and Frenchy will never be welcomed into this circle—they will be discriminated against by these "elites," and will never receive the privileges that "insiders" receive. Of course, the elites will be unlikely to see this as discrimination—they will see their "discrimination" as the careful use of common sense. Bourdieu claims:

> Habitus are generative principles of distinct and distinctive practices—what the worker eats, and especially the way he eats it, the sport he practices and the way he practices it, his political opinions and the way he expresses them are systematically different from the industrial owner's corresponding activities. But habitus are also classificatory schemes, principles of classification, principles of vision and division, different tastes. They make distinctions between what is good and what is bad, between what is right and what is wrong, between what is distinguished and what is vulgar, and so forth, but the divisions [from one habitus to the next] are not identical. Thus, for instance, the same behavior or even the same good can appear distinguished to one person, pretentious to someone else, and cheap or showy to yet another. (Bourdieu 1998, 8)

The members of the wealthy class, or the dominant class in this case, see Ray and Frenchy through the lens of their own habitus and, as such, see them not only as different but as bad or wrong. Their exclusion of such differences are therefore not seen (by them) as arbitrary, but as good and right. Discrimination therefore functions under the mask of *rightness*.

For a social theorist like Bourdieu, one's class in a so-called meritocracy has more to do with one's habitus than one's merit. Or, to put it slightly differently, *what counts as "meritorious" is often one's habitus*.

Each class acquires a habitus that is well suited to a particular class position: blue-collar families train children who "fit" to blue-collar jobs and white-collar families will train children who will "fit" to white-collar jobs, and this will work largely independently of intelligence, work ethic, and so on. No matter how hard Ray and Frenchy attempt to join wealthier classes, they will never be included—their habitus will always be subject to the hysteresis effect and will therefore count against them, in the sense that their habitus will always make them appear to members of wealthier classes as lacking common sense or reason. Frenchy's attempt to "dress up" and look nice for her party was unsuccessful—she didn't have the eye for subtle differences to pull it off. Or, to put it as Bourdieu does in the quote above, what she saw as "distinguished", her guests saw as "vulgar." By contrast, the least intelligent wealthy person may be included as an insider to elite circles because of her habitus. Wealthy people find jobs for those within their network of family and friends—the dumbest member of an elite class could get "placed" in a job that would never be accessible to the smartest poor person in the world. This is not because elites have more intrinsic merit than others, but simply because class habitus is counted as meritorious—which is a privilege ultimately awarded on unfair grounds. As I noted above, social domination through discrimination takes place as if it were right and good, at least from the perspective of those who control jobs and other positions of status.

This sort of exclusion of people with an alternate habitus is linked up with a legitimation of their abandonment. Bourdieu argues,

> The Anglo-American ideology, always somewhat sanctimonious, distinguished the "undeserving poor," who had brought [poverty] upon themselves, from the "deserving poor," who were judged worthy of charity. Alongside or in place of this ethical justification there is now an intellectual justification. The poor are not just immoral, alcoholic and degenerate, they are stupid, they lack intelligence. (Bourdieu 1998, 43)

For Bourdieu this is doubly unfair to those with an alternate habitus: their social subordination is *created* by the way habitus works in the system (they are *seen as stupid* because they have an alternate habitus, and are thus excluded from jobs or positions of privilege), but the system simultaneously *blames them* for their subordination (they did not deserve jobs or positions of privilege *because* they were stupid).

It is for these sorts of reasons that Bourdieu and others argue that class difference can be reproduced over time without anyone intending it to be reproduced. Individuals are socialized into "self-perpetuating hierarchies of domination" (Swartz 1997, 6), and—because of how their habitus works—"actors *unwittingly* reproduce the social stratification order" (Swartz 1997, 7; emphasis added).

Those of us who live in a so-called meritocracy live in a world much more like the medieval social world than we think. Our social hierarchies are not assigned at birth and rigidly reinforced throughout life and without exception, but our social hierarchies are reproduced because of the class habitus we are socialized into from birth. Class movement isn't expressly forbidden and isn't impossible, but class differences are nevertheless largely maintained. We don't check people's literal pedigree in our society, but we do check their "habitus pedigree." The problem for Bourdieu is that the practical difference between these is minimal. Whether I cannot enter an elite class because I was born a serf or because I tell "mom-back" jokes is ultimately immaterial—either way the social hierarchy is reproduced.

Habitus and Religion

How does habitus relate to what we colloquially call religion? A full answer to this question will have to wait until Chapter 8, but at the very least we can say at this point that communities often have their own habitus, even those sorts of communities we call religious.

Because social concepts and categories almost always group together dissimilar things, it is usually impossible to find a set of common elements that every member of a category shares. Unlike most religious groups, many Christians define themselves around a set of beliefs or doctrines, which sometimes makes it easier to find relatively common similarities. Protestants, for instance, tend to have a set of beliefs in common that distinguishes them from Catholics. However, it is not always the case that everyone who self-identifies as part of a Protestant group shares the same beliefs. This is particularly the case with evangelical Christians. Evangelical Christianity—a predominantly American form of Protestantism—has been notoriously difficult to define around a set of doctrines or beliefs because the different groups that self-identify as "evangelical" have had a lot of different beliefs that have changed or evolved over time. Julie Ingersoll, a scholar of evangelical Christianity, notes, "With each attempt at definition, there are inevitable groups that 'seem to be' evangelical but are ruled out, because of some view they hold or some practice they embrace" (Ingersoll 2003,

12). That is, if we line up people who self-identify as evangelical, or who seem to be evangelical, but then posit a definition based on what they seem to have in common, we inevitably end up excluding some of the ones we wanted to include.

It is for this reason that Ingersoll suggests that we should throw out the search for common doctrines: perhaps what is relatively common to evangelicalism is *not* doctrine but a shared habitus. Ingersoll writes (here she is in part quoting Barbara Wheeler):

> Wheeler suggests that observers of evangelicalism consider that "it is not doctrine or ancestry or warm feeling … but religious culture." Maybe, she continues, "the best definition of an evangelical is someone who understands its argot, knows where to buy posters with Bible verses on them, and recognizes names like James Dobson and Frank Peretti." Wheeler points to the distinctly evangelical religious dialect, leaders and celebrities, self-help groups, and Christian service providers (e.g., chiropractors and dentists), as well as the extensive material culture of music, tee-shirts, bumper stickers, books, and jewelry. (Ingersoll 2003, 13)

Ingersoll does not use the term habitus here, but we can see she is talking about the same thing: evangelical Christians have a very distinct dialect and set of tastes.

The evangelical dialect is particularly obvious—it has even been satirized by evangelicals themselves. The Bel Air Drama Department of the Bel Air Presbyterian Church (in Los Angeles, California) has an amusing video on YouTube called "Christianese" (available at www.youtube.com/watch?v=4H-29cJSuv8). The video is set in the format of a television commercial for audiotapes that teach foreign languages. It begins with a scene in which a young woman is with a church group, but doesn't understand the language and phrases the group is using (such as "delve into the Word," "the Lord just put it on my heart," "I stepped out in faith," and "grieve the Holy Spirit"). The narrator says, "Ever been part of a conversation with other Christians and you have no clue what they're saying? Well, no more! Announcing the tape series you've been waiting for: How to Speak Christianese." The narrator goes on to explain that this tape series, which you can listen to "in the privacy of your very own home," will explain what Christians mean when they use these unusual phrases—so that you can avoid the "unwanted embarrassment" that comes with feeling like an outsider. Of course this is an evangelical group satirizing themselves, but they are illustrating one of Bourdieu's key ideas: the way people talk—their diction or dialect—can serve as a social boundary marker that designates some people as insiders and others as outsiders. No doubt this evangelical group is pointing out the exclusionary nature of their diction with the hope of avoiding the exclusion that typically results, but in doing so they are making it obvious that even they recognize the boundary-marking nature of their way of talking.

So perhaps what is relatively common (although not completely common) to most evangelicals is not their doctrines or beliefs but, instead, their diction and their tastes in Christian music, novels, t-shirts, and so forth.

I have family members who have a white, middle-class, *and* evangelical Christian habitus. They include in their circle of friends not only people who think, talk, dress, and behave like them, but they also want what they call "good Christian people." What does that mean? At the very least it means that they want to be around people who share their Christian-inflected habitus. This is relevant for the parts of the country they live in, where evangelical Christianity is a dominant group, and their collusion has wide-ranging effects: if one does not share their evangelical Christian habitus, one will be excluded from certain social circles and job networks. In fact, just as having a visible tattoo or facial piercing might exclude one from certain job possibilities, so to be unable to use an evangelical Christian vocabulary might exclude one from certain job possibilities. "[One's] social sense is guided by the system of ... signs of which each body is the bearer—clothing, pronunciation, bearing, posture, manners—and which, unconsciously registered, are the basis of 'antipathies' or 'sympathies'" (Bourdieu 1984, 241). That is, who one *sympathizes with* or has *antipathy toward* will depend on one's initial read of their habitus. Consequently, when a business owner implicitly wants "good Christian people" among her workers, she needn't explicitly say so or explicitly discriminate—it is just that those people with an alternative habitus will appear wrong, bad, vulgar, etc.—they will elicit antipathy rather than sympathy. On the one hand, when having the "right" habitus is implicitly counted as "meritorious," those with that habitus will experience a wide variety of privileges; those with a shared habitus will be included in the collusion.

On the other hand, discrimination against those with an alternative habitus will happen naturally and invisibly.

We see this sort of privilege and discrimination in the experiences of a young woman named Gina Welch, author of *In the Land of Believers: An Outsider's Extraordinary Journey into the Heart of the Evangelical Church*. Welch is an atheist who went "undercover," so to speak, at televangelist Jerry Falwell's church in Lynchburg, Virginia; she wanted to see what evangelical communities were like from the inside, so she pretended to be an evangelist for a little over a year. At first it was difficult, because she did not understand the evangelical dialect. Eventually, however, she was able to master it:

> I had recently cleared the language barrier, finally unpacking idioms that had signified nothing to me when I first started at Thomas Road [Baptist Church]. Now I knew what it meant to speak in the flesh or the Spirit, I knew what it meant for the Lord to put something on somebody's heart.
>
> (Welch 2010, 114)

Prior to her achievement of an insider's status, she was pulled over by a Virginia highway trooper. The trooper unfortunately looked warily at her California driver's license:

> "I don't know what you're doing here," he said, ripping a ticket off his pad, "but we don't drive like that in Virginia."
>
> Years later I got pulled over running late for [church] one Sunday morning, going 80 coming into Lynchburg from Charlottesville. The trooper again looked at my California license warily and then asked why I was driving so fast. I told him, nerves buzzing, that I was late for church.
>
> "Don't be nervous," he said. "It's alright. Where do you go to church?"
>
> I mentioned Thomas Road [Baptist Church], explained that I drove down on Sundays and Wednesdays. Recognition smoothed his features like a cool cream. "You come down every week ..." he said, smiling and shaking his head in wonder.
>
> He asked me nicely to slow down, then let me go.
>
> (Welch 2010, 99)

It would be inappropriate to make too much of merely two experiences (and Welch admits this), but it is worth noting that this is precisely what we would expect to see if this trooper was an evangelical Christian similar to the ones at Thomas Road Baptist Church: once learning she was an insider (an evangelical) rather than an outsider (a Californian), the trooper registered sympathy rather than antipathy for her and let her go—she was admitted into the collusion.

Subjects do not necessarily "merit" sympathetic treatment by those in the same religious community, but they receive it all the same. And when one religious group is the dominant group in a particular region, their unconscious extension of sympathy to those with a similar habitus and unconscious discrimination against those with a different habitus results in that religious group being indirectly but effectively installed as the ruling group. This can take place even when these subjects are state employees; in a sense, evangelical Christianity becomes the established state religion when employees of the state (like the trooper above) have an evangelical habitus. The discrimination against other religious groups—that is, those religious groups with an alternative habitus—will happen unconsciously and unwittingly. In such cases, religious domination through discrimination takes place as if it were right and good, at least from the perspective of those dominant religious practitioners who are in positions of power.

5

How Religion Works: Legitimation

> [R]eligion is something eminently social. Religious representations are collective representations that express collective realities.
>
> Émile Durkheim, *The Elementary Forms of Religious Life* (2001, 11)

Legitimation

Social order is largely reproduced over time through the cycle of socialization. As noted above, presumably the first person who wore pants did so just because he or she individually liked pants. However, wearing pants has become a fictitious necessity: my parents were taught that they had to wear pants, they taught me to wear pants too, and I'll teach my children that they have to wear pants. Through the process of socialization, social practices reproduce themselves over time.

Socialization doesn't always "take," however, and often people begin to ask "why?" Every once in a while a child asks her parents, "Why do I have to wear pants?" The first answer to the "why" question is usually "just because that's the way things are." This usually works, because people conveniently ignore that when it comes to social constructions, this is completely false: things *are not* just the way they are; things are how we have made them. But most practices have become mystified or naturalized. Wearing pants has become natural to me; I couldn't imagine going to work without pants. Again, there is nothing at all natural about this—many societies throughout time haven't required individuals to wear pants. But the practice has become naturalized *here*, so that it has become a fictitious necessity.

Nevertheless, "Conventions … are likely to be challenged all the time unless their justifying principle can be grounded in something other than conventions" (Douglas 1986, 48). What happens when "that's the way things are" doesn't suffice as an answer? What happens when individuals probe further and require further justifications? This is when societies turn to what scholars call "legitimation." Legitimations offer some sort of justification for conformity to a practice, and they often involve appeals to what the gods say. At the end of Chapter 3 I asked why my grandmother was *forbidden* to wear pants. According to her community, it was "because the Bible says so." "Because God says so" or "because the Bible says so" are obvious legitimations that appeal to divine authorities. A related technical term for what is going on here is "manufacturing consent." People don't always want to do what they are told, but one can manufacture their consent by convincing them that they must, that it's inevitable that they comply, or that there will be supernatural consequences if they do not. Why should we do this? Responses such as "you'll go to hell if you don't" are clearly designed to manufacture the consent of those listening.

This emphasis on how discourses ("discourses" is the technical term for "ways of talking") can be used to legitimate or manufacture consent to social order requires us to switch from thinking about what discourses *mean* and instead focus on how they are *used* or what they *do*. This approach requires us to think about the *social effects* of the way people talk, rather than their apparent meaning. If we focus merely on the "meaning" of "the Bible says so" we'll miss out on the social effect. Literally, the members of my grandmother's community were simply saying that the Bible says women cannot wear men's clothes. But if we focus on the social effect, we might notice that this way of talking also *does* something: it functions to add an additional level of (supernatural) authority to what they were saying.

Because of this focus on the social effect of religious talk, religious stories, religious rituals, and so on, the primary questions we ask will not be "What do they say?," "What do they mean?," or "Do they really believe it?" Instead we will ask, when reading a text, for instance, "Who is trying to persuade whom of what in this text? In what context is the attempt situated, and what are the consequences should it succeed?" (Lincoln 2006, 127). That is, we'll focus on what may or may not be *accomplished* by what is said. In many cases we will find that consent to social order is being manufactured.

Throughout the history of Western civilization there have been many who have suggested that religious legitimation is absolutely necessary for social order. Philosophers like John Locke and Jean-Jacques Rousseau suggested that people would not be moral unless they believed in hell: they argued that morality would not work unless people believed that a god would send them to hell when they died *unless* they acted morally. Consequently, Locke and Rousseau argued in their political writings that atheism should be illegal: atheists will not obey the law because they have nothing to fear in the afterlife. In retrospect, their worry was obviously misplaced; empirical evidence demonstrates that those who identify as atheists do obey the law. However, there is no doubt that some people *do* act morally out of a fear of eternal punishment, so the point remains: religious legitimations can justify certain social norms or practices when people question them. In sum, the social order can be maintained when it is questioned or criticized through the use of religious legitimations. "God says so" or "God will punish you if you don't" are only the most obvious and straightforward examples of religious legitimation. As we will see below, the reproduction of the social order sometimes requires much more complex forms of legitimation or justification; manufacturing consent can be a messy process.

While legitimations can seem like intentional manipulations, this is not necessarily the case. Few scholars in the discipline of religious studies believe that religious people intentionally manipulate others with talk about gods. On the contrary, appealing to gods comes naturally to people who are raised in communities where those sorts of appeals are normal. If one thinks God is good and sexism is bad, one will naturally come to the conclusion that God must be opposed to sexism. If someone is faced with sexist behavior and responds by saying, "God wouldn't approve of that," it is unlikely that that person is trying to intentionally manipulate her audience. Rather, saying this will come automatically and will seem like common sense, even though it is still a religious legitimation of sexual equality. As Bruce Lincoln puts it, "it is often the case that those who would persuade others [by means of legitimation] *are themselves most persuaded of all*" (Lincoln 2007, xv; emphasis added).

In addition, most social theorists are ambivalent about whether legitimation is good or bad. On the one hand, legitimation maintains social order, which usually serves the interests of the population within a community. If we all did what we wanted all the time without any respect for social norms, we would have chaos—and few people's interests are served when chaos reigns. On the other hand, social order can often be oppressive. As noted above, less than two hundred years ago white people in America thought it was entirely appropriate to buy and sell people with dark skin. When others objected, white people in the American south offered a religious legitimation: they insisted that "almighty God created the races" and pointed to passages in the Bible that appeared to justify slavery, of which there were several (see Botham 2009). However, this was obviously an oppressive legitimation. So there is nothing intrinsically good or bad about social order or legitimation—they can be good or bad, depending on the circumstances.

What is the difference between a legitimation and a religious legitimation? For Peter Berger (see Berger 1967, 29ff), a legitimation is religious when it involves some sort of superhuman or supernatural element. If one asks one's boss, "why do I have to do this," and one's boss says, "because it is in your contract," that is a justification designed to get one to comply. For Berger, that's a legitimation, but not a religious one. If one's boss went on to say, "because you'll go to hell if you don't," then it is a religious legitimation, because it involves an appeal to something beyond the human realm. Similarly, Bruce Lincoln says,

> religious claims are the means by which certain objects, places, speakers, and speech-acts are invested with an authority, the source of which lies *outside the human*. That is, these claims create the appearance that their authorization comes from a realm beyond history, society, and politics ... Among these resources figures prominently one that is both a prize and a weapon in such struggles: the capacity to speak a consequential speech and to gain a respectful hearing. With religious claims, the attempt is made to naturalize (indeed, to supernaturalize) this capacity, thereby placing it—and some people's hold on it—beyond the possibility of contestation. (Lincoln 1994, 112; emphasis original)

What Lincoln is suggesting here is that once one's claims are "supernaturalized," so to speak, they get an authority beyond one's own. Appeals to gods, if convincing, carry more authority than appeals to oneself.

However, as David Kertzer notes in his discussion of rituals, this sort of distinction between "religious" and "non-religious" (such as nationalist rituals) is not all that useful. Societies are full of legitimations and rituals of all sorts, and the so-called "religious" ones work in the same way as the so-called "non-religious" ones—there is no substantial difference between the two when it comes to the way they work. "[S]uch a distinction is more a hindrance than a help in understanding the importance of ritual in political life" (Kertzer 1988, 9). Consequently, we will follow Kertzer here: there is no reason to emphasize a distinction between religious and non-religious legitimations, and, on the contrary, it will prove useful to compare them and study them side-by-side.

Cultural Toolboxes and the Maintenance of Social Order

It is useful to think of a culture as a "toolbox" with a wide variety of "tools" inside. "[C]ulture … [is] a profuse repertoire of discourses and practices, that is, what other authors have labeled a 'tool kit,' or a 'surfeit of cultural material'" (Hammer 2009, 10; see also Bayart 2005, 105). These "tools" are what are used to legitimate the social order. Kertzer notes that we do not usually invent these sorts of tools. On the contrary, we inherit them:

> Most often, people participate in ritual forms that they had nothing to do with creating. Even where individuals invent new rituals, they create them largely out of a stockpile of pre-existing symbols. (Kertzer 1988, 10)

> Every culture has its own store of powerful symbols, and it is generally in the interests of new political forces to claim those symbols as their own. (Kertzer 1988, 42–3)

A cultural toolbox—or a culture's "stockpile," to use Kertzer's term—can include all of the following types of tools, to take the example of the American nationalist cultural toolbox:

- *Concepts, norms, and values*—freedom, equality, "the American way," civil liberties, patriotism, "life, liberty, and the pursuit of happiness," "In God We Trust".

- *Traditions, rituals, and practices*—July 4th celebrations (including fireworks, barbecues, etc.), inauguration ceremonies, pledge of allegiance, playing the national anthem at baseball games.
- *Myths and stories*—George Washington cutting down the cherry tree, the ride of Paul Revere, Johnny Appleseed, the story about how dropping "the bomb" in World War II was unfortunate but absolutely necessary to end the war, the myth that America is the "land of opportunity" and a "meritocracy".
- *Texts*—the Declaration of Independence, the Constitution (including the Bill of Rights).
- *Icons*—the eagle, the statue of liberty, the Washington memorial, the Empire State building, Uncle Sam, Lady Liberty.
- *Figures*—Thomas Jefferson, George Washington, Benjamin Franklin, Abraham Lincoln.
- *Ideologies*—"manifest destiny," "common sense".

Most of these tools have an almost universal privileged or authoritative status in America; this is what makes them useful for legitimating the social order. Since the American constitution is authoritative in America, people will appeal to it to justify certain things. However, since the American constitution does not carry any authority in China, it will not be used there to legitimate or maintain the social order. The application of such tools is limited to the reach of their authoritative status.

Elements (or "tools") in cultural toolboxes are frequently used to reflect and reinforce the elements of societies we saw in Chapter 3: (1) insider/outsider boundaries, (2) social positions and social hierarchies, and (3) social roles, moral norms, behavioral codes, and so on. It will be important for us to focus not so much on what these sorts of things *mean*, but more on what they *do*, how they're *used*, or what their *social effects* are:

> one cannot ... study myth, ritual, and/or religion in pristine isolation: rather, we must take careful account of the society in which these are rooted, a society whose structures and organization they continually re-present in accurate and/or mystified terms, and which they usually—but not always—help to perpetuate. (Lincoln 1991a, 173)

Social boundaries

First, *elements of cultural toolboxes can be used to reflect and reinforce social boundaries*. Perhaps the most obvious examples of this are flags: nations use flags to identify themselves. Most ships on the open ocean are required to bear flags of their nation of origin. The Canadian flag on a ship tells the world: *this is a Canadian ship*. Catholics are sometimes known for wearing a crucifix on a chain around their neck; this says to the world: "I'm a Christian." Similarly, evangelical Christians are known for having fish symbols on their car, such as the one in Figure 5.1. This symbol also tells the world: "I'm a Christian." By contrast, some atheists and evolutionists who oppose conservative evangelical Christianity have appropriated this symbol and tweaked it a bit, so that it looks like a fish evolving by growing legs (Figure 5.2). This tells the world that the owner of the car identifies as an insider in another group, and a group that is *opposed* to the Christian group. In short, this symbol tells the world: "I'm outside conservative Christianity and I'm inside the evolutionist camp." In response, the conservative Christians have taken this symbol and manipulated it as in Figure 5.3. This tells the world: "I'm a Christian and I think the Darwinist groups are stupid." Note that all of

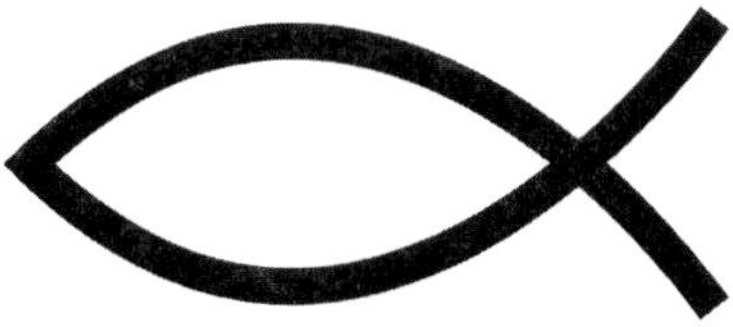

Figure 5.1 Jesus fish.

Figure 5.2 Darwin fish.

Figure 5.3 Jesus fish eating a Darwin fish.

these symbols mark an individual as an insider or a member of a certain group, and simultaneously opposes him or her to another group. From our perspective, what these symbols "mean" is less important than what they do: *they mark insider/outsider boundaries.*

Most of the Lotus Sutra—a famous Mahayana Buddhist text—is about how wonderful the sutra is, a focus that draws insider/outsider boundaries. That is, much of the sutra tries to convince the reader that followers of *this* sutra are better off than followers of *other* sutras. The text even suggests that the preaching contained in the book is the "greater vehicle" to enlightenment, as compared with all those "lesser vehicles" out there. The people who follow these other traditions "fail to understand" (Watson 2002, 26), and one famous historical figure named Shariputra (who was long since dead when the Lotus Sutra was written) is even portrayed as saying that he misunderstood the truth until he heard the "greater vehicle" in the Lotus Sutra:

> How greatly I have been deceived! …
> Formerly I was attached to erroneous views,
> acting as teacher to the Brahmans.
> But the World-Honored One [i.e., the Buddha], knowing what was in my mind,
> rooted out my errors and preached nirvana.
> I was freed of my errors
> and gained understanding of the Law of emptiness [i.e., the teaching of the Lotus Sutra]. (Watson 2002, 27)

To make an analogy with the Christian tradition, this would be like telling a story in which Paul says that he realized that the teaching of the Catholic Church was wrong, and eventually converted over to Protestantism. The way this sort of story works is to take an authoritative historical figure and use him or her as a puppet who says the things one wants him or her to say. The Lotus Sutra is full of stories about the greatest magical things that happen when people read or hear *this* sutra. In fact, the superiority of the Lotus Sutra over other Buddhist traditions seems to be the central theme of the book. In short, *the stories in the Lotus Sutra draw insider/outsider distinctions between different Buddhist groups.*

Rituals too can mark insider/outsider boundaries. For instance, the Catholic Church requires all members to go through what they call "first communion." Communion, also called the "Eucharist," is one of the central ritual practices of the Catholic Church. However, not everyone can participate in communion—individuals can only do so after they have gone through an initiation process. The initiation process involves taking classes on the doctrines of the Church, confessing one's sins to a priest, etc. The final part of the initiation is the ritual celebration of one's "first communion." This ritual is designed to mark an individual as a full insider in the Catholic Church, with all the rights and responsibilities of a full member. Prior to that ritual initiation, there are things one cannot do—in particular, one cannot take communion. People who are not Catholic and have not gone through the ritual do not have the rights of a full member—if they attended a Catholic Church they would not be allowed to participate in the Eucharist (unless they hid their identity as outsiders). In summary, the central function of the ritual is marking one as an insider to the community, rather than an outsider. Again, from our perspective, what is important is less what the first communion ritual "means"—if we asked a Catholic priest he would probably tell us it meant something relating to Jesus' body and blood—and more what the ritual "does": *it marks some individuals as insiders.*

Émile Durkheim once argued that what was fundamental to religion is that it unites all people in a community, giving them a sense of solidarity with one another (Durkheim 2001). On the one hand, this is in part clearly true: people do get a sense of belonging when they participate in a religious tradition. On the other hand, Tim Murphy rightly notes that Durkheim's point is too simple: group membership is about *differentiation* as much as unity.

> [E]ven a casual survey of the history of religions shows that [Durkheim's insistence on unity] is, at best, a half truth. Insofar as religions unite one group, they do so by *differentiating* its members and its memberships from other groups. Difference, not unity, is the dominant trope in the history of religions.
>
> (Murphy 2007, 137)

In addition, not only do religious traditions demarcate insiders from outsiders, but there is always a value judgment in the distinction: "*By definition*, that which the one sees as holy, the other sees as evil" (Murphy 2007, 138; emphasis original). The people with the Darwin fish are not just dividing themselves from conservative Christians; they are criticizing conservative Christians. The stories in the Lotus Sutra do not just draw lines between different forms of Buddhism; they are designating one group as the "great" group and the other groups as "lesser." These are not just neutral insider/outsider distinctions, but asymmetrical valuations.

Social hierarchies

The second point of focus is that *elements of cultural toolboxes can be used to reflect and reinforce social hierarchies and social positions.* Let me offer an example of how a story can do this. There are multiple creation stories in what is called the ancient Hindu tradition. One of them, from the Rig Veda, describes a "primal man" (a giant person with god-like qualities), who was killed and whose body was divided up to make the world.

> 11. When they divided up [primal] Man,
> Into how many parts did they divide him?
> What was his mouth? What his arms?
> What are his thighs called? What his feet?
>
> 12. The Brahman was his mouth,
> The arms were made the Prince,
> His thighs the common people,
> And from his feet the serf were born.
> (Goodall 1996, 14)

This is not just a story about the creation of the world; it is a story that reflects and reinforces a certain class structure. The differences between mouth, arms, thighs, and feet are not just differences. On the contrary, they are hierarchical: the mouth is at the top, and the feet are at the bottom. Similarly, the Brahmans (the priestly class) were made out of the mouth, so they are at the top of society. The serfs (the servant class) were made out of the feet, so they are at the bottom of society.

> Here, as in all such cases, the duties and privileges of the various social classes … are justified ("explained") by reference to their bodily [associations]. ... Warriors fight because of their association to the arms, chest, heart, and lungs (where energy

> and courage are located), while the lower classes run errands, produce food, and generally support their class superiors because of their proximity to feet, legs, and abdomen.
> (Lincoln 1991a, 174)

We should not understand this story as merely reporting on how the world was really created (in any case, we are approaching these things from a sceptical perspective); instead we should understand this story as suggesting how the world *should* look. That is, it is not a "description" or a "map"; it is a "prescription" or a "blueprint." The author is telling us who should have the most authority in society and who should have the least. In addition, the story depicts the social order not as created by humans, but as created by divine beings. Challenges to the social hierarchy are therefore challenges to the divine order of things. So, if we focus on what this story "does" rather than what it "means," we will see the following: *this story reflects and reinforces a certain social hierarchy*. This story makes a fictitious necessity out of an arbitrary social order.

There is a story in the middle of the Lotus Sutra that involves an eight-year-old girl (called the "dragon girl") who achieved Buddhahood very quickly. Of course, her quick Buddhahood was the result of having heard the "greater vehicle" in the Lotus Sutra rather than a lesser one. However, the author of this story has to deal with the fact that in most Buddhist traditions at the time, it was believed that women were inferior to men and could not achieve enlightenment—at least not until they were reincarnated as men. In the dialogue, a man says to the dragon girl,

> But this is difficult to believe. Why? Because a woman's body is soiled and defiled, not a vessel for the Law. How could you attain the unsurpassed bodhi? … [A woman] cannot become a Buddha. How then could a woman like you be able to attain Buddhahood so quickly? (Watson 2002, 86)

The narrator answers the objection by completing the story:

> At that time the members of the assembly all saw the dragon girl in the space of an instant *change into a man* and carry out all the practices of a bodhisattva, immediately proceeding

> to the Spotless World of the south, taking a seat on a jeweled lotus, and attaining impartial and correct enlightenment. With the thirty-two features and the eighty characteristics, he expounded the wonderful Law [i.e., the teaching of the Lotus Sutra] for all living beings everywhere in the ten directions. (Watson 2002, 86; emphasis added)

The story therefore does not challenge the idea that women cannot attain Buddhahood. The story gets around it by saying that she was able to turn herself into a man and *only then* achieve Buddhahood. Rather than challenge the gender hierarchy, the story *reflects and reinforces the superiority of men over women.*

Rituals too are often used to reinforce social hierarchies. A common example is seating patterns. Lincoln draws attention to these in his book, *Discourse and the Construction of Society*. He notes how medieval feasts had seating arrangements that reflected the social hierarchy—each man had a seat in relationship to the king or noble that reflected his distance from the top of the hierarchy. "The map of the [dining] hall is thus also a map of society, in which persons of different rank and standing were assigned to different loci along a north–south axis" (Lincoln 1989, 79). He similarly notes (132) how his own family dinner table was organized to reflect the social hierarchy (Figure 5.4).

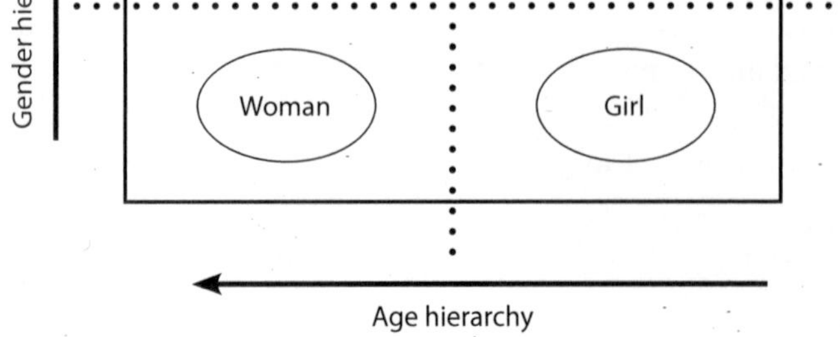

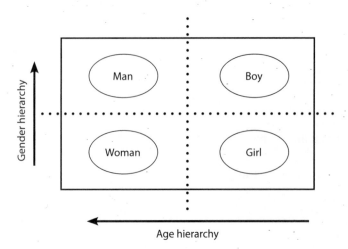

Figure 5.4 The heteronormative family table (adapted from Figure 8.2 of *Discourse and the Construction of Society*, © 1989 Bruce Lincoln).

This seating arrangement reflects two things: gender hierarchies and age hierarchies. On the one side there are males, and on the other side are females. But each side is additionally divided by age: the younger are on one side and the older on another. This accords with my own experience: every big Thanksgiving dinner I have attended has had a separate children's table, distinct from the adults' table. In addition, the seat on the end is almost always occupied by the oldest male present—I have never seen a woman of any age sit on the "throne" end of the table. Similarly, throughout the history of the Christian Church, it has often been the case that the seating in the church was divided by sex (a practice the early Christians appropriated from Jewish synagogues). In addition, churches have also divided seating by race. In summary: *ritual seating patterns reflect and reinforce social hierarchies*. By sitting where they are invited to sit, individuals learn who they are and where they sit in the social hierarchy.

Assigned behaviors

The third and final point of focus is that *elements of cultural toolboxes can be used to reflect and reinforce assigned behaviors: social roles, moral norms, behavioral codes, and so on*. This is perhaps the easiest to understand—Aesop's fables provide a great example. There is almost always a "moral to the story." Readers learn, for instance, from the tortoise and the hare that "slow and steady wins the race." Similarly, Jesus tells a story in the gospel of Matthew in which he says that when the end of the world comes, someone referred to as the "son of man" will judge everyone:

> When the Son of Man comes in his glory, and all the angels with him, he will sit on his throne in heavenly glory. All the nations will be gathered before him, and he will separate the people one from another as a shepherd separates the sheep from the goats. He will put the sheep on his right and the goats on his left.
>
> Then the King will say to those on his right, "Come, you who are blessed by my Father; take your inheritance, the kingdom prepared for you since the creation of the world. For I was hungry and you gave me something to eat, I was thirsty and you gave me something to drink, I was a stranger and

> you invited me in, I needed clothes and you clothed me, I was sick and you looked after me, I was in prison and you came to visit me."
>
> Then the righteous will answer him, "Lord, when did we see you hungry and feed you, or thirsty and give you something to drink? When did we see you a stranger and invite you in, or needing clothes and clothe you? When did we see you sick or in prison and go to visit you?"
>
> The King will reply, "I tell you the truth, whatever you did for one of the least of these brothers of mine, you did for me." (Matthew 25:31–40)

The moral of the story? Whoever helps anyone who needs food, clothes, etc., is *actually* helping Jesus, and those people will be rewarded on judgment day; consequently, Jesus' followers should be doing these things. What this story "means" is that people will be judged in a certain way at the end of time. What the story "does" is to reinforce certain behaviors as good and necessary, specifically by instilling the fear of not doing these things (the next few verses after those quoted above show that the son of man casts the other group into an eternal fire). In summary: *this story reflects and reinforces certain moral norms.*

Sometimes all three aspects of society (i.e., group boundaries, social hierarchies, and social behaviors) can be reflected and reinforced in a single cultural tool. For instance, in Deuteronomy, an ancient Israelite text in the Torah, social boundaries, social hierarchies, and social behaviors are reinforced or legitimated. In this book Moses reports his god's laws to the Israelites. They learn all of the following:

1 Israelites are *insiders*, and Hittites, Girgashites, Amorites, Canaanites, Perizzites, and so on are *outsiders*. Israel is not to make treaties with them, not to show mercy to them in battle, not to intermarry with them, etc. (see Deut. 7). On the contrary, at several points Israelites are encouraged to engage in genocidal warfare with these other ethnic groups ("You must destroy all the peoples the LORD your God gives over to you"; Deut. 7). Israelites are supposed to mark themselves off from these *outsiders* through ritual worship ("You must not worship the LORD your God in their way"; Deut. 12) and through the foods they eat (Deut. 12).

2. Israel is a community replete with different *social positions* differentiating those within the community. There are formal, legal differences between all of the following: Levites and non-Levites (the Levite clan is the priestly class; Deut. 18); slaves and non-slaves (Deut. 15); kings, judges, officials, and other citizens (Deut. 16–17); Israelites and prisoners of war in the community (Deut. 21); first-born sons and other sons (Deut. 21); married individuals and unmarried individuals (Deut. 22); virgin women and non-virgin women (virginity is apparently irrelevant for men; Deut. 22); betrothed women and unbetrothed women (Deut. 22); men who have lost their testicles and men who have not (Deut. 23); ethnically pure descendants and ethnically impure descendants (Deut. 23); men at war who have had nocturnal emissions (wet dreams) and men who have not (Deut. 23); and so on. Note that many of these social positions are non-existent in Western society (e.g., there is no social position assigned to men at war who have wet dreams), and hardly any of these social positions are *formal* in Western society (e.g., there may be a social difference between virgins and non-virgins, but no formal—i.e., legal—rights and responsibilities follow from this difference as they did in ancient Israel).
3. Israel is a community that abides by certain behavioral codes, most of which are linked to the social positions mentioned above. Slave owners are required to behave toward their slaves in certain ways; children are required to behave toward their parents in certain ways; betrothed women are to be treated differently than unbetrothed women; virgins are to be treated differently than non-virgins; and so on. In fact, a large portion of Deuteronomy is dedicated solely to behavioral and moral codes for particular social positions.

This single text does all three of these things: it reinforces social boundaries, social positions and social hierarchies, and behavioral codes. In addition, it adds a supernatural legitimation. Moses, the character who is speaking throughout the book, concludes by noting that those who follow this social blueprint will be blessed: their god will help them conquer their enemies and they will be successful farmers (Deut. 28: 7–8). By contrast, if Israel does not follow this social blueprint, they will be cursed: they will be barren, they will be unsuccessful at farming, their god will make them diseased, their god will send other nations to destroy them, and their god will send men to rape their women (Deut. 28: 15–35). Therefore readers learn that this social order was not invented by humans; on the contrary, it is divinely ordained, and those who violate it will be punished by their god. *This is a powerful way to reinforce or manufacture consent to the social order.*

It is important to note that competing groups within a single society generally use the same cultural tools. For instance, a speech writer for the Democratic candidate for president would use the type of American nationalist cultural tools listed above—perhaps she might throw in a quote from former American President Thomas Jefferson to support her candidate's views. Jefferson is an authoritative figure who carries a weight in America that someone like the former British Prime Minister Winston Churchill would not. However, speech writers for the Republican candidate will use *the same set of tools*. In any particular culture, people generally use the same cultural toolbox—it is just that they use the tools in different ways. When Christians argue among themselves, they generally appeal to the same text: the Bible. However, it is clear that different Christians have used the Bible in different ways: two centuries ago some American Christians appealed to the Bible to legitimate slavery, and other American Christians appealed to the Bible to oppose slavery. The same is true of all so-called sacred texts such as the Torah, the Qur'an, etc. The way the tools in a cultural toolbox are used is always *highly variable*.

Elements of cultural toolboxes (and their uses) are necessary for maintaining social order. Lincoln discusses how something as simple as a marriage ritual is required in order to reproduce a particular type of social order, in part because it involves "the transition of certain core values from one generation to another" (Lincoln 1991b, 114). Although the familial relations are social—we can tell because they vary from society to society—they are usually presented as natural, and thereby reinforced and naturalized in wedding ceremonies.

> [T]he distinctions between married and unmarried individuals, licit and illicit sexual relations, legitimate and illegitimate children, all come into being with and through the performance of wedding ceremonies, without which none of these categories would exist. It is thus insufficient to say that each wedding moves those for whom it is performed from the single to the married state. … [I]t is infinitely more instructive

> to observe that each wedding (as well as each divorce) actually establishes and re-establishes marriage and singleness as meaningful categories of social existence.
>
> (Lincoln 1991b, 114)

For Lincoln, were we to take away marriage ceremonies that sacralize (i.e., make sacred) a certain type of human relationship, those types of human relationships would cease to hold the significance they do. The way in which different familial social positions relate to one another remains stable only insofar as we repeatedly reflect and reinforce them as necessary and natural. Cultural toolboxes (both religious and non-religious) and social order are two sides of the same coin:

> the cosmic and the social sides of this religious ideology … [are] both part of the same system. And one cannot separate the elegant strands of speculative thought from the brutal facts of social hierarchy and exploitation: it was, and regularly is, the persuasive power of the former which makes the latter possible. (Lincoln 1991a, 174)

Maintaining or Challenging the Social Order?

This brings us to a qualification of the idea that legitimations merely maintain or manufacture consent to social order. If different people can use elements of their cultural toolboxes to support different social agendas, does this not mean that the cultural toolbox could be used to support the status quo *and* to challenge the status quo? Or to support some elements of the status quo and challenge others? The answer is an unqualified *yes*.

> [H]umans make their world; they make their world in conditions they inherit which are not all within their control; theoretically, understanding this "making" involves redefining social structures and cultural institutions as not simply given but *constituted* and, hence, as containing the possibility of being changed. (Mohanty 1997, 137; emphasis original)

As Berger and Luckmann argue, "The experts in legitimation may operate as theoretical justifiers of the status quo; [but] they may also appear as *revolutionary* ideologists" (Berger and Luckmann 1967, 128; emphasis added). There is nothing about the tools in a cultural toolbox that predetermines how they can be used—they can be turned toward a variety of different ends. Cultural tools are easily recycled for "new political purposes," and "new political forces eagerly rummage through the preexisting body of religious rituals and symbols" to find those that will work for them (Kertzer 1988, 45).

Similarly, Bruce Lincoln suggests that myths—and I think that he would say the same of all types of cultural tools—

> may be instrumental in the ongoing construction of social borders and hierarchies, which is to say, in the construction of society itself. As such, myth has tremendous importance and is often a site of contestation between groups and individuals whose differing versions of social ideals and reality are inscribed within *the rival versions of the myths they create.* (Lincoln 1991a, 123; emphasis added)

That is, different groups can tell different versions of the same myth (or practice different versions of the same ritual, etc.) in order to accomplish *different* social ends. As a result, "Studies of myth ... ought to be attentive to the multiple competing voices that find expression in differing variants, and to the struggles they wage in and through mythic discourse" (Lincoln 1991a, 124). By telling persuasive stories that depict the world the way they think it should be, groups can fight and defeat other groups without raising a fist or shooting a gun. For Lincoln, myths and rituals are often best understood as bloodless battlegrounds for social power. (It was for this reason that Lincoln gave up trying to find the "original" meaning of different myths—their social power lies in their revisions and retellings, not in their origin.) David Kertzer concurs:

> Rituals do change in form, in symbolic meaning, and in social effects; new rituals arise and old rituals fade away. These changes come through individual creative activity. People, in short, are not just slaves of ritual, or slaves of symbols, they are also molders and creators of ritual. It is because people create and alter rituals that they are such powerful tools of political action. (Kertzer 1988, 12)

The elements of a cultural toolbox do not have a fixed use; they are often capable of being recycled by individuals who take them up and give them new life. Anthropologist Marshall Sahlins points out that concepts, signs, or words—which we usually think of as having stable uses that are outside our power to change—are necessarily subject to change when they are put to work in specific contexts: "*in action* ... cultural categories acquire new functional values" (Sahlins 1987, 138; emphasis added; see also Williams 1977, 39ff, and Bayart 2005, 114). There is nothing to guarantee that a word is used in exactly the same way each time it is repeated, and without such a guarantee, it automatically follows that to repeat a word is necessarily to put it at risk of change. Just as cars will break down the more we drive them, so words will change meaning the more we use them in new contexts. The same general rule applies to all elements of cultural toolboxes. If cultures are capable of evolving, if cultural tools are capable of being reused in new ways, it follows that they can be used to challenge rather than reinforce the status quo.

In addition, not only can the use of cultural tools change, but so can the *selection* of which tools will be utilized. There is always a great deal in the repertoire of a tradition, and not all of it can be used at once. As Raymond Williams puts it:

> tradition ("our cultural heritage") is self-evidently a process of deliberate continuity, yet any tradition can be shown, by analysis, to be a selection and reselection of those significant received and recovered elements of the past which represent not a necessary but a *desired* community.
>
> (Williams 1981, 187; emphasis original)

That is, what elements from a cultural toolbox people choose to utilize will depend not on the tradition itself, but on what they *desire* their communities to look like. Because of this, the idea that tradition reflects the *past* is misleading; the selective uses of tradition reflect what people want for their *future*.

Kertzer points out that a number of rituals were used by American revolutionaries to challenge rather than reinforce the status quo (i.e., America's status as a colony of England). They made effigies of King George III and burned them, had funerals for them, and buried them

(Kertzer 1988, 161–2). He suggests that these rituals may have been more effective at generating negative sentiments toward the king and England than did the signing and distributing of the United States' constitution. He calls these "rituals of revolution," and it is clear that they have a great ability to challenge rather than reinforce the social order.

Let me offer two other examples. In America, most heterosexual Christian weddings end with the minister announcing the married couple to the audience like this: "I now present to you Mr and Mrs Craig Martin." In a small but substantial way, this reinforces the subordination of women's social position to that of men. Where is the wife's identity in this? Not only does her last name disappear, so does her first name. It seems as if she as an individual becomes nothing more than an attachment to her spouse. In much of the history of Western culture, this has been the case: women have often been little more, socially speaking, than a fashion accessory. In order to challenge this social subordination of women to men, when my wife and I got married we asked the minister not to do this, so he announced us in this way: "I now present to you Craig and Erica." In this way we were attempting to tweak the ritual in order to challenge the status quo, rather than reinforce it. (It is worth noting that we still placed my name first, which is still subtly patriarchal.)

Second, it is a ritual in North America for a man to ask a woman to marry him, rather than the other way around. Again, this is an odd sexist practice if we are aiming at gender equality. As a result, when I proposed to my wife I told her that I was not, by asking her to marry me, agreeing to marry her—I asked that she propose to me as well. So, a few weeks after I proposed, she reciprocated by proposing to me in return. Again, in this way we were attempting to tweak a social practice in order to challenge the status quo, rather than reinforce it.

There is nothing unusual about this. Tools such as hammers can be used for hammering or pulling out nails, but they can also be used for purposes for which they were never intended: one could use a hammer as a doorstop. How the available tools in a cultural toolbox will be used depends in part on tradition—people will tend to use them in the ways they have always been used—but when circumstances change they can turn the tools to entirely new uses, or even reactivate old tools that have not been used for a while.

It is for this reason that sophisticated social theorists insist on the ambivalent nature of these things: they are neither good nor bad in themselves. Bruce Lincoln is right in his discussion of some rituals that reinforce the subordination of women:

> First, ... rituals are involved not only in the construction of persons, but also in the construction of categories of persons, and in the construction of the hierarchic orders in which categories and persons alike are organized. Second, ... such processes are not neutral, but have their victims, as well as their beneficiaries. And third, ... *those victims have the means—creative and powerful—to react against the processes that victimize them*. Among these are the disruption of existing rituals and the creation of novel rituals.
>
> (Lincoln 1991b, 119; emphasis added)

In summary, the tools in our cultural toolbox can be used to reflect and reinforce social boundaries, hierarchies, and prescribed behaviors, but they can also be used in order *to challenge and reshape* these things.

Religious Essentialism

Having a cultural toolbox is like having a box of Legos. With a box of Legos one could build just about anything. There's nothing intrinsic to the blocks themselves that predetermines how they will be used. One could build a car, a plane, a hat, a cat, or whatever. Similarly, the elements of a cultural toolbox can be used to maintain (or challenge) all sorts of different types of society. The elements of the Christian cultural toolbox have been used both to support violence and to oppose violence. The elements of the Islamic cultural toolbox have been used both to maintain sexism and to challenge sexism. The elements of the Hindu cultural toolbox have been used both to maintain the elite privileges of the priestly class and to challenge the elite privileges of the priestly class. No matter how such cultural tools have been used in the past, someone will probably use them in new ways in the future. In short, *there are no essences to be found in a religious tradition's cultural toolbox.*

One reason why it is hard to see this is that it conflicts with a naïve theory of religion many people hold. People often take religion to be about "beliefs," and then assume that the actions or behavior of religious practitioners is caused or informed by their beliefs. They tend to think of the beliefs as the essence of a religion, and assume that the essence unfolds in the same way for all religious practitioners. This is not only false as a theory of religion, but it is a dangerous theory as well: it leads to people thinking that if the Qur'an says Muslims should kill infidels, that means people who "believe" in the Qur'an will kill infidels. This is clearly not true. Malory Nye puts it well in his discussion of how defining religion as a "belief system" slides into an explanatory account:

> What is happening here is, in fact, that this idea of belief is being used not merely as a definition [of religion], but as an explanation. That is, religious belief becomes an explanation in itself: our absence of understanding what a person from another religion is doing or thinking leads us to fall back on our basic knowledge of their beliefs. Thus we assume that a Hindu is acting a certain way because s/he 'believes' in reincarnation, and a Muslim in another way because s/he believes in Allah. Such an explanation may or may not be correct—but what it does is rule out a number of other possible explanations. (Nye 2008, 117)

It may be the case that beliefs directly inform practitioners' behavior some of the time, but often the reverse is true: people's stated beliefs are legitimations that reflect and reinforce an already existing set of behaviors, practices, or agendas. The naïve theory of religion supposes that practices and behaviors follow directly from beliefs, but in fact "beliefs" are often invoked secondarily.

In *Politics, Law and Ritual in Tribal Society*, Max Gluckman discusses an African nation in which the citizens believed that whoever became king of their nation was awarded supernatural powers (after going through a ritual that instantiated him as king); it was believed that these supernatural powers were so great that he could control even the weather. However, because he was thought to be capable of controlling the weather, "the king was held responsible for what we would call 'natural' disasters, and rebellion against him was warranted in the national interest" (Gluckman 1965, 165). That is, sometimes after a natural disaster the citizens would rebel and overthrow the king for causing or failing to prevent the disaster. The naïve theory of religion would approach this sort of story and assume that the people obviously have to rebel because of their beliefs—as if the day after the disaster they said to themselves, "well, I don't want to do it, but my belief system says I've got to overthrow the king." But Gluckman rightly points out that the "belief" didn't work this way. Gluckman (1965, 165) writes, "in practice rebellion was probably waged by a prince as leader *of a discontented faction*" (emphasis added). That is, the people didn't feel the need to rebel every time a natural disaster happened, but only when a rebellion *was already brewing*. People were not at all forced by their beliefs to depose a king after a natural disaster; rather, discontented groups who *already opposed the king* sometimes used natural disasters to legitimate the rebellion they wanted to launch for independent reasons. It is not that their beliefs determined their rebellion, but that their rebellion already in the works was legitimated by an appeal to their beliefs.

If we set aside the naïve theory of religion, according to which beliefs always inform behaviors—like an essence that unfolds from the inside out—it is much easier to see that beliefs and doctrines are usually in a very complex relationship with behaviors and practices, and that people who share a cultural toolbox may in fact do very different things with the tools inside. Rather than try to discover an essence to a religious tradition by looking at its cultural toolbox (like trying to prove that Christianity is intrinsically a violent religion because Jesus said "I came to bring not peace but a sword"), we can better understand the social effects of myths, rituals, and other elements of cultural toolboxes if we consider the critical questions listed above *in particular historical contexts*: In this particular historical context, who is trying to persuade whom of what by brandishing this element of the cultural toolbox? What are the consequences should the attempt succeed? Is domination being reinforced or challenged? Answers to these sorts of questions will bring into relief a wide variety of things we would not otherwise notice.

In conclusion, it is important to note that those things colloquially called religious traditions are *not simply* direct and intentional tools of legitimation. Raymond Williams, a Marxist social theorist who writes about literature, puts it well:

> if we are asked to believe that all literature is "ideology," in the crude sense that its dominant intention (and then our only response) is the communication or imposition of "social" or "political" meanings and values, we can only, in the end,

> turn away. … [I]t is really much simpler to face the facts of the range of intentions and effects, and to face it as *a range*.
> (Williams 1977, 155; emphasis original)

While Williams is talking about literature, the same is true of those things we call religious traditions: it seems clear that legitimation of social order is sometimes intended and sometimes not, and that sometimes legitimation is an effect even when it is not intended. There are a range of intentions and a range of effects, and it would be foolish to assume otherwise. We would seriously oversimplify things were we to completely reduce religion to intentional legitimation.

6

How Religion Works: Authority

Authority and Projection

Appeals to authority are almost universally found in religious traditions. When people ask the "why do we do it this way?" question and demand an answer, the answers offered—designed to manufacture consent—are almost always linked to locally authoritative figures, texts, icons, symbols, and so on. We say "locally authoritative" because *none* of these things are authoritative for all societies in all times and places. What is authoritative here may not be authoritative there, and what is authoritative now may not have been authoritative then.

There are at least three types of authority. First, there are authoritative *things*: texts, rituals, practices, and so on. The US constitution is clearly an authoritative text in the United States. The Bible is an authoritative text for Christians. Zazen—a type of meditation—is an authoritative practice for Zen Buddhists.

A second type of authority is linked to religious *figures* or social *positions* above one in a social hierarchy. For instance, the Dalai Lama is an authoritative figure for Tibetan Buddhism. The pope is an authoritative figure for Catholicism. The president is an authoritative figure in the United States. For those who claim to be adherents to these traditions, the actions or commands of these authoritative figures have a special, important, or sacred status. US citizens aren't expected to follow what the president of Iran says, but they are expected to respect the authority of the American president. The same goes for authoritative figures in religious social hierarchies.

The authority of figures in a social hierarchy is almost always maintained by some set of visual markers or social practices. In the military, subordinates have to salute superiors; in addition, every military person wears insignia that designates her place in the social hierarchy and whether she bears authority over others. US presidents do not have authoritative status as president until they pass through a swearing-in ceremony. One minute before being sworn in, Barack Obama was *not* president; one minute after, he *was* president. This sort of ritual is not just window dressing—it is fundamental to establishing a figure's authority. When President Kennedy died in 1963, his vice president—Lyndon B. Johnson—knew that he wouldn't carry the authority of a president until he was sworn in. Consequently, on the plane ride from Dallas, Texas (where Kennedy was shot) back to Washington, DC, Johnson was sworn in. In addition, he had Kennedy's widow—Jackie Onassis—witness the swearing-in ceremony. Johnson was smart—he knew that once this was announced upon his arrival in DC, it would solidify his position as the new president (see Kertzer 1988, 57ff). Similarly, the pope's hat is not worn for fashion reasons, but to mark his place at the top the social hierarchy.

A third type of authority—the most important type, arguably—involves *absent* authority figures. Examples of absent authority figures would include gods, saints, bodhisattvas, and other types of divine or dead figures. Gods and goddesses, Jesus, the Buddha, Krishna, and similar figures are different from the former type of authoritative figures because they are, in some important way, *absent*. If one has the right connections, one could call up the Dalai Lama, the pope, or the US president, and ask them what they think about particular social or moral issues. By contrast, one can't call up Jesus and ask him what he thinks. If one attributes a view to the Dalai Lama that he doesn't hold, he can challenge it or contest it; he can always hold a press conference and publicly declare: "I *did not* say that!" Absent authority figures cannot do that. The so-called "founding fathers" of the United States are authoritative figures, but they are dead and therefore absent. If one says they were in support of separation of church and state or against separation of church and state, there is pretty much nothing they can do about it—they are absent.

Authoritative texts, insofar as their authors are absent, are very similar to absent authority figures: people can offer interpretations of a text, but if the author is gone, the text is open to continual interpretation and reinterpretation. Neither dead figures nor authoritative texts can contest the views attributed to them. For this reason we can consider absent authority figures and authoritative texts side by side in what follows.

Because absent authority figures and texts with missing authors cannot contest the views attributed to them, they are more open to what scholars call "projection." In a sense, projection is just like ventriloquism: when ventriloquism takes place, a ventriloquist projects her voice onto a dummy—making it seem as if her voice is actually coming from the dummy. Similarly, religious practitioners will often project their own views on absent authoritative figures or authoritative texts, which they effectively use as dummies. These absent authoritative figures make good dummies precisely because they're *absent*—they are not around to contest the words being put into their mouth.

Why would someone project their views on an authoritative figure? The answer is simple: these figures carry more *authority* than most other people do. If John Doe tells Jane Doe that she should support gay rights, she probably wouldn't much care—John Doe is nobody of importance. However, if Jane is a Buddhist and John can convince her that the Buddha would support gay rights, that would carry a lot more authority. If she is a Muslim and he could convince her that Allah would support gay rights, that would carry a lot more authority. In short, most religious practitioners are nobodies—but their words can be made to carry a great deal of authority if they can successfully put their words into the mouth of an absent authority figure.

That projection takes place is undeniable. The figures of the Buddha and Jesus provide us with perhaps the best examples. In the Buddhist tradition, an indefinite number of sutras (i.e., teachings) are attributed to the Buddha. The Lotus Sutra, for instance, begins with the following narration: "At that time the World-Honored One [i.e., the Buddha] calmly arose from his samadhi [i.e., a type of meditation] and addressed Shariputra, saying: 'The wisdom of the Buddhas is infinitely profound and immeasurable[']" (Watson 2002, 1). The rest of the sutra is narrated as a conversation between the Buddha and his audience. However, the text is almost definitely dated at least a few centuries after the Buddha died. There are thousands of similar sutras; they were written after the Buddha died, but pretend to offer the actual words of the Buddha himself. In *The Invention of Sacred Tradition*, Olav Hammer and James Lewis point out that almost all religious traditions falsely attribute texts to absent authority figures. "Why does nearly every religion have spurious traditions and misattributed texts?" (Hammer and Lewis 2007, 4). Their own answer is that attributing texts to a founder or other ancient figure "confers legitimacy to religious claims and practices" (Hammer and Lewis 2007, 4). Their book offers evidence that this sort of falsification has happened in Scientology, Mormonism, Christianity, Zoroastrianism, Judaism, and various forms of paganism. "The authority gained by projecting one's tradition into a legendary past … can serve several purposes. … [In part], inventing one's history enables religious innovators to shape the tradition of which they are part by ascribing at times radically new ideas to ancient, founding figures" (Hammer and Lewis 2007, 6). That is, innovations are passed off as if they were ancient, thereby giving them an air of authority they might not otherwise have had.

How about Jesus? Not only do many scholars believe that many of the words attributed to Jesus in the New Testament did not originate with him, but it is clear that throughout history various "interpretations" of those words in the New Testament have involved projection. About a hundred years ago Albert Schweitzer (1910) wrote a book called *The Quest of the Historical Jesus* in which he surveyed a series of nineteenth-century biographies of Jesus. What did he find? They all reflected nineteenth-century values. More recently a scholar named Jaroslav Pelikan (1985) wrote a book called *Jesus through the Centuries* in which he surveyed views of Jesus from the first century to the present. Stephen Prothero (2003) wrote a book called *American Jesus: How the Son of God became a National Icon* in which he surveyed the views of Jesus from the beginning of the United States to the present. Olav Hammer (2009) edited a volume on *Alternative Christs* that surveyed a wide variety of visions of Jesus outside so-called orthodox Christianity. All of these works found that in every time period, people remake Jesus in ways that reflect the social, moral, and political concerns of their own age. Glancing at only a few examples will "show how the interests of each epoch are echoed in emerging alternative Christ themes" (Hammer 2009, 280). Take a few minutes to surf the web, or go down to a local bookstore, and see how many different books you can find about Jesus. It turns out that Jesus supports just about every social, moral, and political position imaginable. There are books that portray Jesus as a communist, and there are books that portray Jesus as a capitalist. There are books that portray Jesus as against gay rights, and there are books that portray Jesus as supporting gay rights. Whatever social, moral, or political position one can find, someone has probably written a book saying that Jesus would support that position. Logically speaking, Jesus simply could not have held all these positions—and perhaps not any of them, since they all concern nineteenth-, twentieth-, and twenty-first-century issues, and Jesus lived in the first century. That Jesus has been made to support contradictory social positions is absolute proof that *projection has to be taking place at least some of the time*. The reason for this is quite clear, as Bart D. Ehrman suggests:

> [V]ery few people who devote their lives to studying the historical Jesus actually *want* to find a Jesus who is completely removed from our own time. What people want … is *relevance*. If Jesus was completely a man of his own time, with a world view and a message totally out of sync with our own materialist, postcolonialist, secular-humanist, or whatever-ist society, then he may be an interesting historical figure, but he is scarcely relevant … to the issues and concerns that people need to confront today. And so it's no wonder that some scholars—who are human after all—want to make Jesus into something else—a proto-feminist, or a Neo-Marxist, or a countercultural Cynic.
>
> (Ehrman 1999a, 127; emphasis original)

Projection often takes a very specific form, which scholars call a "return to origins" narrative. A return to origins narrative involves positing a "pure" origin of a religious tradition, which was followed by a "corruption" of the original message. The narrative is used to authorize one's own position as "pure" while portraying one's opponents' position as "corrupt." According to Prothero, this strategy is a central means Christians use to make their religious reforms seem as though they were what was originally intended by Jesus:

> That strategy begins with a bold refusal. It starts when a religious reformer refuses to equate Jesus with the Christian tradition. The religion *of* Jesus, the reformer asserts, is not the same as the religion *about* Jesus; and what really matters is what Jesus did and taught. The second step is to isolate certain beliefs or practices in the Christian tradition as unreasonable or antiquated or immoral. The next step is to use

> the cultural authority of Jesus to denounce those beliefs or practices as contrary to true Christianity—to call for religious reform. (Prothero 2003, 41; emphasis original)

That is, people make this sort of equation: "my religion is the religion *of* Jesus *himself*, but your religion is a religion *about* Jesus—therefore mine is good, original, and pure, whereas yours is degraded and inauthentic." What is ironic, however, is that just about every Christian group uses the exact same strategy to criticize other Christians—they all say "*we've* got the true, original Jesus; *you've* got a corrupt, bastardized version." By claiming that their own view is a return to the "origin" or to the "true message" of Jesus, they get to use his authority to legitimate their own reforms.

Most people have seen a Rorschach inkblot, such as is shown in Figure 6.1. This is how Rorschach tests are supposed to work: the idea is that a psychologist will show an inkblot to a patient and ask her what she sees—her answer is, theoretically, supposed to shed light on what's going on in her unconscious mind. If one says, "I see myself stabbing my mother to death with a knife," then the psychologist has probably discovered something interesting about one's unconscious desires. What the patient "sees" in an inkblot theoretically tells us more about the patient than it does about the inkblot itself.

Similarly, much of what religious practitioners say about absent authoritative figures tells us more about *them* than it does about the authoritative figures themselves. If a Buddhist practitioner claims that adherence to the message of the Buddha demands that we give equal rights to gays and lesbians, this probably tells us a lot more about *the practitioner's views* than about the Buddha himself. When people ask themselves "What would Jesus do?," their answer is pretty much always the same as the answer to the question "What do *I think* I should do?" The same goes whether we're talking about the Buddha, Jesus, Allah, Avalokiteshvara, Krishna, or whomever.

One group of scholars writing about projection points out that many people see religion as providing a "moral compass" of sorts; gods are assumed to be sources of "ultimate moral authority" (Epley et al. 2009, 21,537). However, they also note that "The central feature of a compass ... is that it points north no matter what direction a person is facing. This research suggests that, unlike an actual compass, inferences about God's beliefs may instead point people further *in whatever*

Figure 6.1 Rorschach inkblot (© 2011 Kathleen Roepken, reproduced with permission).

direction they are already facing" (Epley et al. 2009, 21,537; emphasis added).

Is projection intentional? That is, do religious practitioners *intentionally manipulate* their audiences by projecting their values onto authoritative figures? It would be naïve to suggest that projection is *never* intentional, but it seems unlikely that it is intentional most of the time. In fact, it appears that most people are unselfconscious and unreflective about the rhetoric they use. Interpreters develop what Pierre Bourdieu calls a "practical sense," which allows them to intuit the stakes of religious debates and negotiate them by responding in ways that both reflect their prior assumptions and serve their future interests (see Chapter 4). For Bourdieu, one's practical sense is "second nature," and, as such, arguments are executed naturally, without hesitation, and without conscious reflection.

From the assumptions that the Bible is good and that sexism is bad, it is a short leap to the conclusion that the Bible must be opposed to sexism. Similarly, other interpreters can easily come to alternative conclusions if their practical sense is predisposed to different assumptions: "God made men and women fundamentally different, so wouldn't it follow that God wants men and women to have different social roles?" From this assumption it is a short leap to the conclusion that the sexist social roles prescribed in some parts of the Bible rightly reflect the way God intended the world to function optimally. While some might argue that this is an overly cynical view, there is no other way to account for the great number of fundamentally opposed "interpretations" that can come out of a single figure or text. In any case, this way of accounting for the differences in interpretation need not assume that devotees manipulate their traditions knowingly or intentionally—most of the time projection is performed *unreflectively*.

The figure of Jesus has often been co-opted for Marxist and socialist projects. Many socialist Christians write as if Jesus were a card-carrying communist. Lyman Abbott, a socialist Christian writer from the late nineteenth century, provides us with a clear example of projection in his *Christianity and Social Problems*. There Abbott explains that slavery gave way to feudalism in the Middle Ages, and that feudalism gave way to capitalism in the modern period. Under the capitalist economic system, there arose a sharp class distinction between capitalists and laborers. What should Christians make of this state of affairs? "The general effect of Christ's teaching, and of human development under its inspiration, is to abolish the class distinction between capitalist and laborer, as other class distinctions have been abolished" (Abbott 1899, 163). Although he has already told his reader that the class distinction between capitalists and laborers *did not exist* until the modern period, he projects this Marxist position onto a first-century Jesus. To be fair to Abbott, we should note that he deploys the strategy of projection not to serve his own selfish interests or to bring about some sort of repressive social control—he seems genuinely to intend to bring about social effects that would relieve some of the burdens of poverty. Nevertheless, his interpretation is obviously projective. Abbot's interpretation of Jesus tells us more about Marxist values than it does about Jesus himself. Jesus is possibly the ultimate Rorschach test.

Gandhi provides us with an example of projection in the Hindu tradition. Many Hindus revere the ancient Indian text called the Bhagavad Gita as authoritative, and Gandhi himself seemed to like the text, since he wrote a book-length commentary on it. The Gita is pitched as a dialogue between an Indian god named Krishna and a warrior named

Arjuna. If we consider the Gita in its social and political context, it appears to have been written for the Indian warrior class. The message of the book is complicated, but one of the themes repeated throughout is that warriors must do their warrior-duty and fight. At the beginning Arjuna shows a great deal of reluctance to fight in a particular battle, and Krishna insists over and over that he must fight. Krishna says, "Why this cowardice in time of crisis, Arjuna? The coward is ignoble, shameful, foreign to the ways of heaven" (Miller 1986, 31). He goes on:

> Look to your own duty;
> do not tremble before it;
> nothing is better for a warrior
> than a battle of sacred duty.
>
> The doors of heaven open
> for warriors who rejoice
> to have a battle like this
> thrust on them by chance.
>
> If you fail to wage this war
> of sacred duty,
> you will abandon your duty
> and fame only to gain evil.
> (Miller 1986, 36)

Krishna's conclusion? "Fight the battle!" (Miller 1986, 47).

However, one of the most commonly known things about Gandhi is that he was opposed to violence. In fact, he was one of the pioneers who developed non-violent means of resistance (which were later appropriated by figures like Martin Luther King, Jr.). How could Gandhi reconcile his love of a book telling warriors to fight battles with his commitment to non-violence? It was pretty easy: Gandhi suggested that the themes related to warfare and the injunction to fight were only *metaphors*: the author of the Gita was really talking about the sorts of mental battles individuals fight in their own heads. People often struggle with conflicting desires. For instance, someone might struggle with whether to tell a friend the truth about an ugly outfit or to tell the friend a white lie to protect his or her feelings. This is a superficial example, but that is the sort of "battle" Gandhi suggests the Gita is talking about.

He explicitly states, "We shall leave aside the question of violence and nonviolence and say that this work was written to explain man's duty *in this inner strife*" (Gandhi 2000, 27; emphasis added). Gandhi reconciles his love of the Gita and his commitment to non-violence by projecting onto the Gita what he wants it to say: it is not about *real* violence, it is just about mental battles. In this case Gandhi's interpretation of Krishna's message in the Gita tells us more about Gandhi than about the Gita itself.

It is worth noting at this point that authority is a rather complicated matter and it is too simple to talk as if "authority" were some magical property that simply resides in a figure or a text. When we say that things, people, or absent figures are authoritative, we do not want to imply that there is something special about them in and of themselves. The Torah is not an authority *by itself*—it is authoritative only for a community that recognizes it as authoritative. There are billions of people in the world who do not hold the Torah to be an authoritative text, and it probably means little to them. The Torah's authoritative status is not rooted in the Torah itself, but in the community that gives it sacred status.

Because authoritative status is not derived from the thing itself but from the community that reveres it, anything could, in principle, be given authoritative status. There once was a famous Christian saint named Simon Stylites, who stood on a pillar in the desert praying to his god. He was so respected by the neighboring communities that his feces was given a sacred status—they would collect it from where it dropped from the column on which he prayed. They took his feces and made it into medallions. It is not often that feces is turned into something sacred or authoritative, but the fact that it can be shows us that the authoritative status of a thing is not in the thing itself, but in the community that reveres it as such.

Because authority is not intrinsic but rather conferred by a community, it can best be understood as a relationship between multiple elements. Consider textual authority: the authority of a religious text is an effect produced by the relationship between a *text*, its *interpreters*, and various *audiences*. Were interpreters or audiences to cease to exist, there would be no such thing as textual authority. So when we say that projection reinforces the authority of a text, this means that the work of the interpreter (1) assumes that a particular audience respects a text, (2) appeals to what the text says—or what it can be made to say with ventriloquism—in order to direct the behavior of the audience, and (3) in doing so reinforces or naturalizes the audience's continuing respect for the text.

The reason for drawing attention to this function of authority is because authoritative texts and figures can be utilized by interpreters to direct the behavior of their audiences without the critical reflection of their audiences. It is often the case that interpreters can make invisible their role in the triangular relationship between interpreter, a respected text, and an audience that respects the text. Audiences misrecognize the meaning given by the interpreter as residing in the text itself, and the active contributions of the interpreter to the "meaning" of the text may remain invisible indefinitely. In other words, *projection works only when an audience cannot tell that projection is taking place*. I can manipulate you by projecting my words onto the figure of Buddha only if you cannot see that that is what I am doing—if you knew I was projecting, you would stop listening to me. Most of the time, it seems, projection *does* remain invisible. Interpreters of sacred texts are usually better than magicians at hiding their sleight of hand. As a result, in a sense "authority … is primarily in the hands of those who control the texts" (Rothstein 2007, 27). When an audience's behavior can be directed by a skilful interpreter who invisibly manipulates a text the audience reveres, the authority of the text is simultaneously the authority of the interpreter.

In addition, there is a circular relationship here between projection and authority. People would project their values onto Jesus or Buddha, for instance, only if those figures were widely hailed as authoritative. However, doing so perpetuates within the community the idea that they should listen to what Jesus or Buddha has to say. The strategy of projection reinforces the authority of whatever is subjected to projection (Figure 6.2). Even though the power of the authority of a figure or a text is, in a sense, passed on to its interpreter, it remains the case that the authority of that figure or text is reinforced. Even if the Marxist's interpretation of Jesus persuades her audience to support socialism, *the audience still thinks it is following Jesus* rather than Marx. Projection both assumes and further reinforces the authority of whatever is being subjected to projection.

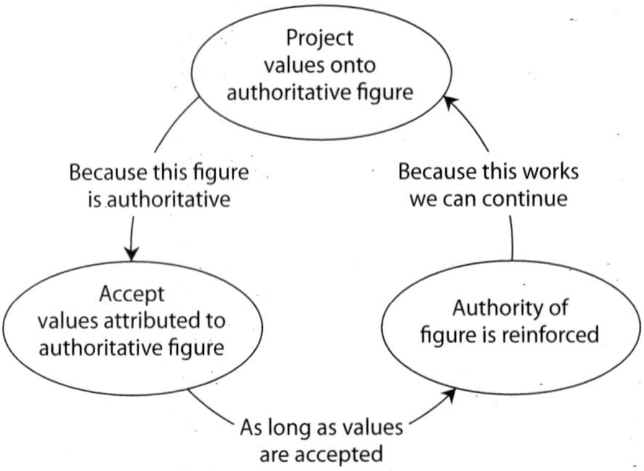

Figure 6.2 The circular relation between authority and projection (© 2011 Valissa Hicks, reproduced with permission).

Selective Privileging

One of the tricks that comes with using authoritative figures or authoritative texts is that sometimes they say more than one wants them to say. For instance, texts like the Bible or the Qur'an sometimes resist projection, simply because there might be parts of them that *contradict* the message one wants to project onto them. When interpreters run up against passages in their authoritative text they don't like, they tend to select and privilege other parts of the text.

Michael Cook points out how this often works with modern Muslim interpreters of the Qur'an. He notes (as did Bart D. Ehrman above) that religious practitioners are interested in authoritative texts because of what contemporary *relevance* they can be made to have:

> The text needs to be interpreted because, having been composed a long time ago … it now contains much that is at first sight obscure, irrelevant, or disconcerting. This means that the commentator has a tendency to approach the text with the presuppositions and concerns of his own time, and may seek to realign the meaning of the text accordingly. Rarely is he concerned to answer a strictly historical question of the form: "Never mind what this means to us now, what exactly did it mean to them then?" (Cook 2000, 28)

From a scholarly standpoint, looking at how a text was understood in its original context is completely different from looking at how a text has been recycled over time in other contexts. Because religious practitioners want to make old texts relevant for their own times, they will privilege those parts of the texts that are easier to fit to their own presuppositions, or those parts of the texts onto which they can most easily project their own views.

Cook shows how this is the case with interpretations of the Qur'an on the question of religious tolerance. What does the Qur'an say about whether Muslims should tolerate people in other religions? Cook points out that it actually says *multiple* things. On the one hand, there is what Cook calls the "sword verse":

> [W]herever you find the idolaters, kill them, besiege them, wait for them at every lookout post; but if they turn [to God], maintain the prayer, and pay the prescribed alms, let them go on their way, for God is most forgiving and merciful.
>
> (Haleem 2004, 116)

According to this passage, people who worship other gods (which are merely idols, according to the Qur'an) should be killed unless they convert to Islam. There is, however, a qualification in the same section for Jews and Christians, who are called "the People of the Book": "Fight those of the People of the Book who do not [truly] believe in God and the Last Day, who do not forbid what God and His Messenger have forbidden, who do not obey the rule of justice, until they pay the tax and agree to submit" (Haleem 2004, 118). Apparently, idolaters are to be slain, but Jews and Christians will only be required to pay a tax or a fine—although if they do not pay they should be fought by Muslims. However, Cook rightly points out that "these two verses do not represent the full range of Koranic statements bearing on the question" (Cook 2000, 35). In an entirely different section of the Qur'an we find this passage, which Cook calls the "no compulsion" verse: "There is no compulsion in religion: true guidance has become distinct from error, so whoever rejects false gods and believes in God has grasped the firmest hand-hold, one that will never break" (Haleem 2004, 29). According to this passage, the difference between truth and falsehood is obvious, so there is no sense in forcing people to join Islam. Cook points out that the "sword verse" is the one privileged by Muslims who are militant about Islam. By contrast, for most contemporary Muslims—who are not militant—the "no compulsion" verse is "literally a godsend, scriptural proof that Islam is a religion of broad and general toleration" (Cook 2000, 35). One famous interpreter of the Qur'an, Sayyid Qutb, utilized the "no compulsion" verse to demonstrate that Islam was the original religion of toleration. Despite the fact that Qutb was himself a militant, he insisted that "[f]reedom of belief … is fundamental to human rights, and it was Islam that first proclaimed this value" (Cook 2000, 35). Even a militant can interpret the text in a liberal fashion. Whatever the text says about toleration depends in part on what the reader wants it to say—there is enough ambiguity that one can wrestle out of it the message one wants.

The Bible is very much the same. In the Bible the Israelites' god tells them to conquer a number of cities filled with idolaters, and to kill every living thing in those cities. That is, they are not to show mercy even to women or children, as some ancients wanted to do:

> [W]hen the Lord your God gives them over to you and you defeat them, then you must utterly destroy them. Make no covenant with them and show them no mercy. Do not intermarry with them, giving your daughters to their sons or taking their daughters for your sons, for that would turn away your children from following me, to serve other gods. Then the anger of the Lord would be kindled against you, and he would destroy you quickly. But this is how you must deal with them: break down their altars, smash their pillars, hew down their sacred poles, and burn their idols with fire. (Deuteronomy 7:2–5)

In a nearby passage the Israelites' god tells them to beware psychics and false prophets:

> If prophets or those who divine by dreams appear among you and promise you omens or portents, and the omens or the portents declared by them take place, and they say, "Let us follow other gods" … you must not heed the words of those prophets or those who divine by dreams; for the Lord your God is testing you.… But those prophets or those who divine by dreams shall be put to death. (Deuteronomy 13:1–5)

Palm readers and fortune tellers should beware—the Bible says they should be put to death.

These sorts of rigorous demands are present in the New Testament as well. To begin with, in the Sermon on the Mount Jesus insists that his followers must keep following the laws prescribed in the Hebrew scriptures; in fact, he says they have to follow the law *more closely* than they have been. Jesus explicitly states, "whoever breaks one of the least of these commandments, and teaches others to do the same, will be called least in the kingdom of heaven" (Matthew 5:19). So, according to Jesus, those demands made on the ancient Israelites—such as the demand to kill idolaters—are still in place.

In addition, Jesus makes absolute oppositions between following him and every other commitment one might make—and there are serious consequences for falling on the wrong side. In the gospel of Luke, Jesus says his followers must hate their family members: "Whoever comes to me and does not hate father and mother, wife and children, brothers and sisters, yes, and even life itself, cannot be my disciple" (Luke 14:26). In the gospel of Matthew, Jesus says: "I have come to set a man against his father, and a daughter against her mother, and a daughter-in-law against her mother-in-law; and one's foes will be members of one's own household" (Matthew 10:35–6). Throughout the gospels Jesus makes it clear that if one does not follow his teachings, there will be a severe penalty: "You that are accursed, depart from me into the eternal fire prepared for the devil and his angels" (Matthew 25:41). One of Jesus' teachings in Matthew is that one should avoid not only adultery but also lust—so much so that it is better to cut one's eye out rather than commit an act of lust:

> You have heard that it was said, "You shall not commit adultery." But I say to you that everyone who looks at a woman with lust has already committed adultery with her in his heart. If your right eye causes you to sin, tear it out and throw it away; it is better for you to lose one of your members than for your whole body to be thrown into hell. (Matthew 5:27–29)

Jesus' followers have a choice, then, between hell or losing an eye. Jesus did not come to "play nice"; on the contrary, he says, "Do not think that I have come to bring peace to the earth; I have not come to bring peace, but a sword" (Matthew 10:34).

However, as should be obvious at this point, whether Christians privilege these violent passages in the Bible or something much more amenable to contemporary values—like the "love your neighbor" passages—will depend on what Christians want the Bible to say. Many people claim to take the Bible as "literally" true in all respects, but none of them hate their father or mother, and none of them have cut off pieces of their body (although there was a famous rumor that circulated in ancient Christianity that Origen—one of the church fathers—cut off his genitalia because he believed they were causing him to lust). Instead, even people who claim to take the Bible as "literally" true actually choose to privilege more agreeable passages and ignore these more difficult ones, as *all* religious practitioners do.

An open letter to the conservative Christian radio talk-show host "Dr Laura" circulated on the internet a few years ago, and it highlights very clearly and humorously an example of selective privileging. The anonymous author of this letter states the following (which I quote in full):

> Dear Dr Laura,
>
> Thank you for doing so much to educate people regarding God's law. I have learned a great deal from your show, and I try to share that knowledge with as many people as I can. When someone tries to defend the homosexual lifestyle, for example, I simply remind him that Leviticus 18:22 clearly states it to be an abomination. End of debate.
>
> I do need some advice from you, however, regarding some of the [other] specific laws and how to best follow them.
>
> a) When I burn a bull on the altar as a sacrifice, I know it creates a pleasing odor for the Lord (Leviticus 1:9). The problem is my neighbors. They claim the odor is not pleasing to them. Should I smite them?
>
> b) I would like to sell my daughter into slavery, as sanctioned in Exodus 21:7. In this day and age, what do you think would be a fair price for her?
>
> c) I know that I am allowed no contact with a woman while she is in her period of menstrual uncleanliness (Leviticus 15:19–24). The problem is, how do I tell? I have tried asking, but most women take offense.

d) Leviticus 25:44 states that I may indeed possess slaves, both male and female, provided they are purchased from neighboring nations. A friend of mine claims that this applies to Mexicans, but not Canadians. Can you clarify? Why can't I own Canadians?

e) I have a neighbor who insists on working on the Sabbath. Exodus 35:2 clearly states he should be put to death. Am I morally obligated to kill him myself?

f) A friend of mine feels that even though eating shellfish is an abomination (Leviticus 11:10), it is a lesser abomination than homosexuality. I don't agree. Can you settle this?

g) Leviticus 21:20 states that I may not approach the altar of God if I have a defect in my sight. I have to admit that I wear reading glasses. Does my vision have to be 20/20, or is there some wiggle room here?

h) Most of my male friends get their hair trimmed, including the hair around their temples, even though this is expressly forbidden by Leviticus 19:27. How should they die?

i) I know from Leviticus 11:6–8 that touching the skin of a dead pig makes me unclean, but may I still play football if I wear gloves?

j) My uncle has a farm. He violates Leviticus 19:19 by planting two different crops in the same field, as does his wife by wearing garments made of two different kinds of thread (cotton/polyester blend). He also tends to curse and blaspheme a lot. Is it really necessary that we go to all the trouble of getting the whole town together to stone them? (Leviticus 24:10–16) Couldn't we just burn them to death at a private family affair like we do with people who sleep with their in-laws? (Leviticus 20:14)

I know you have studied these things extensively, so I am confident you can help.

Thank you again for reminding us that God's word is eternal and unchanging.

Your devoted disciple and adoring fan.

What this author clearly points out in this satirical letter is that Dr Laura selectively focuses on the passages on male sexuality while blatantly ignoring the surrounding passages. Whether or not Jews or Christians focus on the heterosexist passages probably depends not on something intrinsic to the text but rather on the norms or political preferences of their own community. Selective privileging permits one to sort through authoritative texts and find what one wants to find.

Challenging Authority

Regnant authorities are often subjected to challenge, particularly when they are being utilized to legitimate social agendas that works against some group's interests. There are at least three different ways one could challenge a regnant authority:

1 one can point to competing authorities,
2 one can offer internal critique, or
3 one can offer external critique.

First, one could challenge authority simply by calling into question the self-evident privilege accorded to that authority, especially when there are *competing* authorities. Why, for instance, should I follow Jesus rather than Zoroaster? Why should I follow the New Testament rather than the Zend Avesta? Are there good reasons for following one god rather than another?

The philosopher Jean-Jacques Rousseau was one of the best at pointing out some of the problems with appealing to authority. In one of his books we can hear his own voice coming out through one of his fictional characters, who says the following:

> I considered all the different sects that reign on earth and accuse each other of falsehood and error, and I asked, "Which one is right?"
>
> "Mine!" answered everyone. "Only I and those who agree with me think rightly; everyone else is mistaken."
>
> "How do you know that your sect is the right one?"
>
> "God said so."
>
> "And who told you that God said so?"

> "My minister. He knows. He told me to believe it, and I do. He assures me that those who say anything different are liars, so I do not listen to them." (Rousseau 1983, 271–2)

However, insofar as ministers disagree with one another, which ones should people trust? Rousseau's character goes on to challenge his imagined debate partners, and they respond:

> "God himself has spoken; listen to his revelation."
>
> "That is another matter. God has spoken! What an impressive statement! To whom has he spoken?"
>
> "To men."
>
> "Then why have I heard none of his words?"
>
> "He has told other men to report them to you."
>
> "I understand: it is men who will tell me what God has said. I would rather have heard God himself; it would have been no more difficult for him, and it would have protected me from being misled."
>
> "He protects you from it by proving that his spokesmen were really sent by him."
>
> "How does he prove that?"
>
> "By miracles."
>
> "Where are those miracles?"
>
> "In books."
>
> "Who wrote those books?"
>
> "Men."
>
> "And who saw the miracles?"
>
> "Men who attest to them."
>
> "What! Always human testimony! Always men who report to me what other men have reported! How many men there are between God and myself!" (Rousseau 1983, 273)

Rousseau's conclusion is that determining which authorities to trust tends to depend not on evidence (because the evidence is always handed down by other authorities), but rather on accident of birth: if one is born in a Christian country one will probably trust the Bible, and if one is born in a Muslim country one will probably trust the Qur'an. For Rousseau, accident of birth is not a very reliable way of determining which religious traditions are true.

Rousseau's critique calls authorities into question on the basis of the fact there are so many of them: why would we trust some and not others? This is a serious challenge to taken-for-granted authorities. How does one really know one is not worshipping the wrong god? And, perhaps, how does one know there are any gods at all?

The second type of challenge to authority is what scholars call *internal critique*. Internal critique involves the identification of tensions or contradictions *within* a figure's message or *within* the message of a particular text. In the Bhagavad Gita, for instance, the god Krishna says "I exist in all creatures," but then goes on to say the opposite: "all creatures exist in me, but I do not exist in them" (Miller 1986, 67, 83). Which is it? Does he exist in all creatures or does he not? In the gospel of Luke, Jesus tells his disciples at one point, "whoever is not against you is for you," but then goes on to suggest the opposite principle: "whoever is not with me is against me" (Luke 9:50, 11:23).

These contradictions may not be all that significant, but there are more serious ones one could point to. In the New Testament, Paul says in his letters to the Romans and the Galatians that Christians need not follow the Jewish law. By contrast, in the gospel of Matthew, Jesus adamantly insists that his followers must uphold the Jewish law:

> Do not think that I have come to abolish the law or the prophets; I have come not to abolish but to fulfill. For truly I tell you, until heaven and earth pass away, not one letter, not one stroke of a letter, will pass from the law until all is accomplished. Therefore, whoever breaks one of the least of these commandments, and teaches others to do the same, will be called least in the kingdom of heaven; but whoever does them and teaches them will be called great in the kingdom of heaven. (Matthew 5:17–19)

Many readers misunderstand this because it is followed by a passage where Jesus appears to reverse the meaning of several laws. However, the following "you have heard that it was said [in the Jewish law] … *but I say*" passages always follow a similar form: Jesus says "you have heard," but then goes on to require his followers *not only* to follow the law described, *but* to follow it *even more strictly* than is literally required. For instance "you have heard" that adultery is wrong, "but I say" that even lust is wrong; or "you have heard" that murder is wrong, "but I say" that even anger is wrong.

So Jesus' message is the opposite of Paul's: Paul says Christians don't have to follow the Jewish law (he even condemns those who want to try), whereas Jesus says his followers must not only follow the Jewish law, but must follow it more strictly than the letter of the law requires. Pointing out this substantial contradiction within the message of the New Testament (i.e., this *internal critique*) could constitute a rather serious challenge to the authority of the Bible.

The third type of challenge to authority is what scholars call *external critique*. External critique involves weighing the value of a text or a figure's message against some external criterion. Internal critique would compare, for instance, one part of a text to another part within the same text, whereas external critique would compare the text to something outside the text altogether. Hector Avalos provides us with a stark example of external critique of the Bible. Avalos points out all of the following:

1 The description of the creation of the world in the Bible is contradicted by almost all forms of modern scientific inquiry (Avalos 2009, 50; Avalos 2007, 17).
2 At some points the Bible recommends genocidal practices, which is clearly morally wrong (Avalos 2009, 50).
3 Much of the Bible is patriarchal in its orientation and recommendations, and patriarchy is clearly morally wrong (Avalos 2007, 18).

In each instance the critique is external: Avalos appeals both to scientific research and ethical norms *outside* the Bible to critique the Bible. Every once in a while external critique is simply dismissed by religious practitioners; if a group believes the Bible is entirely divine, then the patriarchal stuff in there must be right, even if it appears wrong to others (if that is their view, internal critique is more likely to gain traction, since internal critique points out contradictions *within* the text itself).

While most uses of authority are designed to legitimate or challenge social order, so are most challenges to authority linked to contestations of social order. For instance, as feminism started to gain ground in the nineteenth and twentieth centuries, we saw the rise of feminist critiques of the Hebrew scriptures and the New Testament. These feminists have used all three types of critique concerning the Bible: they have suggested that the Bible should not even be considered an authority, they have suggested that its comments about women are internally contradictory, and they have suggested that moral norms outside the Bible (such as the norm of gender equality) shows that the Bible is morally wrong, at least where it supports patriarchy.

It is worth noting that if no one were reading the Bible in support of patriarchy, feminists would not care about it; there are millions of patriarchal old texts that feminists ignore because no one finds them to be authoritative today. We should always consider religious claims in specific contexts: who is trying to persuade whom of what, and with what practical consequences should they succeed? The same is true about challenges to authority; to understand "what's going on here" we need to ask similar questions: who is trying to critique what authority, before what audience, and what practical consequences would result were they to succeed? In the case of feminist critiques of the Bible, the answers are fairly clear—the Bible has been and continues to be used to legitimate patriarchal relations of domination, and by criticizing that tool of legitimation, feminists hope to challenge patriarchy.

How do people respond to challenges to their sacred authorities? On the one hand, they could simply dismiss or ignore the challenge. In fact, this is probably what most people do. How does one know it is right to follow the Buddha as opposed to Muhammad, or Ahura Mazda as opposed to Yahweh? Most people ignore the objection and take it for granted that the authorities they have inherited from their parents are the most trustworthy ones.

However, if religious practitioners want to take more seriously criticisms of their authorities, how might they respond? A common response is wishful thinking. Let me offer just one example. When I was a freshman in college I took an introductory course on the Bible, and was introduced to the fact that there are two conflicting accounts of Goliath's death in the Hebrew scriptures (cf. I Samuel 17 and II Samuel 21). Undaunted by what I took to be only an *apparent* contradiction, I quickly raised my hand and suggested that perhaps it was possible that "Goliath" was a common nickname for big and tall men in ancient Palestine; if that were the case, there may have been many Goliaths running around back then, and different accounts of the death of Goliath were not really contradictory but simply the accounts of two *different*

Goliaths. Such speculation, of course, originated not in my informed knowledge of ancient Near Eastern languages, cultures, and practices (I had no informed knowledge of these matters), but in my *wish* that these stories did not conflict with one another. I resolved the contradiction with *wishful thinking*—in my mind they were not contradictory because I did not want to believe they could be contradictory.

Wishful thinking is often a response to these sorts of challenges to authority. If one *wants* to believe that the Bible is perfect, my speculation that there were two Goliaths might be persuasive—despite the fact that there is no justification for this interpretation other than that we *want it to be true* (that is, there is no historical evidence whatsoever for this reading of the text). If one *wants to believe* that Jesus should be trusted over Muhammad, or that the Zend Avesta should be trusted over the Bible, Rousseau's objections are unlikely to make a dent in one's wishful thinking.

Another response to internal critique is projection; for instance, religious practitioners can project onto an apparently contradictory passage in a text the meaning they want it to have. This can work for either internal critique or external critique. If someone points out that Jesus and Paul contradict one another when it comes to whether Christians should follow the Jewish law, one could project onto Jesus' claim the meaning one wants it to have. As noted above, in Matthew, Jesus says "Do not think that I have come to abolish the law or the prophets; I have come not to abolish but to fulfill." Many Christians latch on to the "to fulfill" part and project onto that what they want it to mean. They argue something like the following: "When Jesus says he came to 'fulfill' the law, he meant that he wants to offer us forgiveness of our sins, so that we can be forgiven without having to follow the law." However, this interpretation makes no sense, particularly given the surrounding comments about how very important it is to continue following the law. One could resolve this contradiction between Jesus' and Paul's messages only by projecting onto Jesus' sayings what one wants him to say.

Projection is sometimes a response to external critique as well. The Hebrew scriptures, the New Testament, the Qur'an, the Hindu scriptures, the Buddhist scriptures, etc., *all* have sexist elements. Many of them have violent passages as well—such as the command to kill idolaters in the Qur'an and the Bible, or the command to fight wars independently of whether or not the war is justified in the Bhagavad Gita. Independently of ethically objectionable elements, all religious traditions have *weird* things in them as well—such as Jesus' recommendation in Matthew 19 that some of his followers become eunuchs (that is, a male whose testicles have been removed). These sexist, violent, and weird things may not pose a problem for internal critique (maybe these sacred authorities are *consistently* sexist, for instance, so that there is no internal contradiction), but because of widely accepted Western values—which are *external* to these authorities—many contemporary practitioners find these things to be rather objectionable or problematic. As a result, they may project onto a text a more domesticated meaning. For instance, Gandhi's projection of a meaning onto the Bhagavad Gita was a way for him to reconcile it with his modern ethical values.

Another response to external critique could be partial *rejection*: many religious practitioners reject part of their tradition as outdated, outmoded, or just plain wrong in some respects. For instance, I once met a theologian who said that he accepted Jesus' ethical teachings, but rejected Jesus' claims about the fact that the end of the world was near. Since this sort of rejection is partial, practitioners can save the authoritative figure or text in general.

Finally, we should consider a very specific type of rejection: the *refusal to extrapolate*. What is extrapolation? Extrapolation consists of taking a specific principle, idea, or rule in a text and attempting to fit it to an alternative context. Extrapolation asks: "perhaps this text meant this for them, but they lived in a different context—how can we make this relevant for our own context?" One example of extrapolation is provided by the ways in which the shari'a (the body of Islamic jurisprudence) is interpreted, with respect to rules about fermented drinks. The shari'a forbids the consumption of fermented drinks made from grapes and dates. However, the shari'a says nothing explicit about the consumption of vodka or rum. In order to see the injunction as also applying to vodka or rum, one must extrapolate from a principle assumed to be present in the rule. For instance, one could argue that what is essential to the rule is the prohibition of foods or drinks that have incapacitating effects on one's body and mind. Although it doesn't mention vodka in the injunction, vodka is one such drink that has incapacitating effects. As a result, one could *extrapolate* that the injunction should cover vodka in addition to wine made from grapes.

Unlike extrapolation, which attempts to make some part of a text relevant in an alternative context, a *refusal to extrapolate* attempts to undermine any possibility of extrapolation. Rather than say "how can we make this relevant for our own context?," the refusal to extrapolate attempts to show something like the following: "the context in which this text was written was so different from our own context that there is nothing in it that is relevant for us any longer." This mode of interpretation links the text so radically to its context of authorship that any attempt to draw contemporary relevance is foreclosed. In sum, the refusal to extrapolate says: "this part of the text is past its expiration date."

J. W. Rogerson's *According to the Scriptures* (2007) catalogs two thousand years of Christian uses of this interpretive strategy, each case of which was designed to nullify the continuing authority of the Jewish law. Most of the refusals to extrapolate Rogerson considers involve a universal/particular or essential/inessential distinction, whereby some parts of the Jewish law were categorized as universally applicable, and other parts were categorized as useful for a particular time and place, but no longer. Rogerson shows that St Augustine, for instance, distinguished between *moral* commandments and *ceremonial* laws, and suggested that the latter were not universally applicable.

Similarly, Richard Hooker (1989) makes a distinction between *necessary* and *accessory* laws, and Richard Baxter (2000) distinguishes between *essentials* and *customs*; for both Hooker and Baxter, the former applied universally, while the latter did not. In each case, the deployment of this sort of distinction allowed the interpreters to maintain the authority of the Bible in general, while rendering inconsequential those specific passages that were met with disapproval. (Of course all such refusals to extrapolate ignored Jesus' insistence that the law must continue to be followed.)

How can one tell which parts of the law apply universally and which need not apply any longer? Usually with respect to wishful thinking: Christians tend to sort the parts of the Jewish law into the two categories based on what they *want*. If a Christian group is sexist, then the sexist laws are "universally applicable." If a Christian group's values reflect twenty-first-century Western values, then the sexist material will probably be understood as being "inessential," and therefore no longer relevant. Christians can read the laws and refuse to extrapolate whatever they want to reject.

One might think that the refusal to extrapolate challenges the authority of the text, but it does not. Although the refusal to extrapolate suggests that some part of a text may no longer be applicable, given that circumstances are rather different from those of the original audience, this mode of interpretation separates out some part of the text as irrelevant or no longer applicable, *in contrast with* the other parts of the text that *are still relevant* and still applicable. The text retains its authority, but some parts of it apply only in certain circumstances. This interpretive move is necessary for those who do not want to dismiss the applicability or authority of a text altogether. For instance, many people are willing to dismiss the authority of the text: some people are free to say, "I don't care what the Qur'an says about sex, marriage, gender, homosexuality, or whatever—I derive my moral norms on these matters from other sources." Those who perform a refusal to extrapolate typically do so because they cannot say this. In effect, their position is usually the following: "the Qur'an is still an important authority; it is just that this small part of it is no longer applicable." In adopting this position they get to have their cake and eat it too—the text remains authoritative and parts of it remain applicable, but they can reject those parts they are uncomfortable with. In summary, the refusal to extrapolate deals with challenges to the authority of a text by rejecting one part of the text as out of date, while simultaneously upholding the authority of the text in general.

Authority Is Complicated

In conclusion, authority is an extremely complicated matter. Although religious practitioners frequently hold particular figures or sacred texts as authoritative, that doesn't mean they follow their authorities in any simple or straightforward manner. On the contrary, authorities are often subjected to projection, selective privileging, partial rejection, the refusal to extrapolate, and so on. Knowing who or what some group holds as authoritative tells us *almost nothing* about them—further investigation into how religious groups use or manipulate the authorities they hold dear is necessary to understand religious practitioners. Bible scholar William Arnal is absolutely correct when he suggests that understanding "the historical Jesus"—that is, the actual Jesus behind the myths, legends, and interpretations—is completely irrelevant for understanding Christianity:

> The ultimate goal of historical Jesus studies is to uncover the origins of Christianity itself, to reconstruct the Jesus who is assumed somehow to lie behind this movement as its root *cause*. … [However], ultimately, the *historical* Jesus does not matter, either for our understanding of the past, or our understanding of the present. The historically relevant and interesting causes of the development and growth of the Christian movement will be found, not in the person of Jesus, but in the collective machinations, agenda, and vicissitudes of the movement itself. (Arnal 2005, 76–7; emphasis original)

That is, understanding Christianity does not really require us to understand who Jesus really was, but how the figure of Jesus—as an absent authority—was recreated and recycled over and over in various historical contexts. The reinventions of Jesus are more important than Jesus himself. The same goes for all religious traditions: the "origin" of a religious tradition is largely irrelevant. Religious traditions are subject to ongoing recreation and evolution, and focusing our studies on their "origin" is as misguided as trying to measure the height of an oak tree by looking at an acorn.

7

How Religion Works: Authenticity

> Need it be said that determining the criteria for what is or is not "authentic" is always problematic?
>
> Jean-François Bayart, *The Illusion of Cultural Identity* (2005, 78)

> All that is solid melts into air.
>
> Karl Marx and Friedrich Engels, *The Communist Manifesto* (1998, 38)

In 1553, in the city of Geneva, the theologian Michael Servetus was put to death by being burned at the stake. What had he done to be sentenced to this horrible fate? Was he a murderer? A rapist? A thief? He was none of these things: Servetus was put to death for suggesting that the doctrine of the trinity—the belief that the Christian God, Jesus Christ, and the Holy Spirit are all united as one being—was untrue.

What is the trinity? In the sixteenth century, the three largest branches of Christianity in western Europe (the Catholic Church, the Lutheran Church, and the Reformed Church) all held that God, Jesus, and the Holy Spirit were united in one being. The official doctrine was that all three were divine, but that *couldn't* mean that their church worshiped three different gods—somehow these figures were three *and* one at the same time. The city of Geneva (where the Reformed Church was in league with the city authorities) convicted Servetus of a capital crime for calling this belief into question. His doubt—and his attempts to talk to others about it—made him a *heretic*: someone *who pretended to be Christian but really wasn't.*

John Calvin, one of the founders of the Reformed Church, requested that the sentence of stake-burning be commuted to beheading, but the city refused. On the 27th of October in the year 1553, Michael Servetus was tied to a stake and burned.

Why does Servetus's fate matter to us in the twenty-first century? Servetus's story is just one example of an issue that still has incredible relevance to how religion is used today: the way that the internal unity or internal conformity of a religion is defined and enforced. Or, put another way, it is how religious people answer this question: *Who is like me?* Who is *really* Christian? Or Jewish? Or Hindu? Because of how the Reformed Church in Geneva answered this question—who was *really* Christian and who was not—Michael Servetus was killed. Alleging that someone is *not really* Christian—is not really like me—is a game that sometimes has, quite literally, grave consequences. Although we will focus in this chapter on the example of Christianity, this question applies to all religious traditions.

Who Is a True Christian?

It is not surprising that some of the people who self-identify as Christians don't always get along with other people who identify themselves as Christians. The same is true for any religious tradition: there are pagans who disagree with pagans, Muslims who disagree with Muslims, and Scientologists who disagree with Scientologists. When there are disagreements between different Christians—especially when the stakes are high—it is not unusual for one group to say about the other: "they're not *really* Christian."

What are we to make of these sorts of claims? How could we go about figuring out who is and isn't actually a Christian? It's harder than it looks at first glance. The problem seems to be that every Christian group has their own criterion that they use to determine their group boundaries.

For example, early in the twentieth century, a group of Christians rallied around what they called the five "fundamentals" of Christianity—which is where the term "fundamentalism" comes from. They believed that one is not a Christian unless one believes that Jesus was divine, that Jesus' mother was a virgin, that Jesus' body rose from the dead, that the Bible was historically accurate in every one of its claims, and that

Jesus' death on the cross covers the debt of sin. At the other end of the spectrum, the "death of God" theologians of the 1960s and 1970s identified as Christian, but completely rejected the idea that God existed. One of their battle cries was "God is dead; long live Jesus Christ!" For them, "God" was an authority figure no longer of use to the Christian tradition, which was actually about the message of liberation and compassion spread by Jesus of Nazareth.

So we have two different groups, both of which call themselves (or "self-identify" as) Christian. But where the one group thinks that belief in God, the virgin birth, the resurrection, etc. are necessary for Christian identity, the other thinks belief in God is dispensable—and may even be harmful—for Christians who want to get at the true heart of Christianity, which is compassion and justice. Meanwhile, most contemporary evangelical Christians think a "born again" personal experience is central to Christianity, many Catholics believe that participation in the Catholic mass is satisfactory, and others identify as "culturally Christian" because they grew up in a Christian community and celebrate Christian rituals and holidays, even though they reject all of Christianity's supernatural beliefs. *Almost every group that identifies as Christian uses different criteria for group membership.*

So what do we do? How do we define the borders of a religion? (Obviously we are coming close to some of the issues discussed in Chapter 2; that is, how do we determine membership in category or classification?) One possible solution: to create what scholars call a "stipulative definition."

A stipulative definition is a working definition that helps to narrow down a complicated field for a limited purpose. For instance, a scholar might say something like this: "*For the purposes of this book*, we are using the term 'Christian' to refer to those groups who believe that Jesus is the messiah." Think about it this way: if one were writing a book on "country music," one would have the problem of delimiting what exactly would count as "country music." Would one include John Lee Hooker, Bob Dylan, Neil Young? Would one include the modern, electric-guitar-driven, pop-oriented country, or restrict it to acoustic guitars and traditional instruments? Would one include the indie rock sub-genre "alt-country"? How would one separate country music from folk music? Or from rock music, blues, or bluegrass? Different people use the term differently, and there is no definition that one could give that would fit with all of the different uses out there in the world. But one *could* give a stipulative definition: "*For the purposes of this book*, when we say 'country music' we are referring to music that has the following features ..."

When scholars set out a stipulative definition of "Christian," their stipulative definition never matches up perfectly with all of the different uses of the term employed by those who self-identify as Christian. So a stipulative definition may be pragmatically useful—it may fit *most* who self-identify as Christian—but, as a stipulative definition, it does not go so far as to suggest that this is what Christianity *really is*.

Since stipulative definitions do not claim to define what something really is, they won't help us provide an answer to the question "Who is a true Christian?" And, in any case, Christians who make claims about who is a true Christian probably don't care about stipulative definitions—the leaders of the city of Geneva were not suggesting that Michael Servetus didn't fit their stipulative definition of "Christian," they were saying that he was *not really a Christian*. And to accept their definition would be to cooperate with not only their perspective, but the particular configuration of power that they want to implement in the world. To understand what is going on in these sorts of identity claims we will have to consider *power*.

Power Plays

For centuries, religious practitioners have claimed a special power or special authority for *their* own beliefs and practices by claiming that they have the *real* or *authentic* ones. This sets up a *binary opposition* between "the real" or authentic and "the unreal" or inauthentic—between an "us" and a "them." The contrast between "authenticity" and its opposite lines up with all the other pairs of words that people use to distinguish what they think is real from what they think is false or illegitimate:

- right/wrong,
- good/bad,
- true/false,
- real/fake,
- orthodox/heretical,

and so on. It is important to note that these are not *neutral* distinctions; the words on the left have a positive ring to them, and the words on the right are negative. When we apply these labels, something deeper than just description is happening: we are giving things a value, expressing how they make us feel and how we think they should make others feel.

We see the same sort of strategy with words in many things we do in our culture, even ones not typically labeled as "religious." During the 2008 US presidential election campaign, some members of the Republican Party talked a lot of talk about "real Americans" or "the real America." One of John McCain's strategists, Nancy Pfotenhauer, even made reference on CNN to "the real Virginia," basically meaning those parts of Virginia that agreed with her and her candidate. Every once in a while, when I am facing off with scholars who don't share my views, I might say that their work is "not *really* scholarly." The rhetorical or persuasive effect of the claim to authenticity is basically the same: "My practices or views are authentic—*the right ones*—and these others are inauthentic—*the wrong ones*."

What people usually do not do in such cases is provide an argument for or defense of their claim. In fact, the claim that one's own group is authentic usually gets brought out when the person or group making the claim *doesn't have a good argument*—people resort to what practically amounts to name-calling when they do not have any substantial justification for what they are saying.

Interestingly, this power play can do two different things. On the one hand, as we have seen, it can be used to award a special authority to one's own group: "We are the good group; we have the right interpretation and the real truth. They are the bad group: corrupted, fallen, and false." By claiming that their own group is "authentic," people assert their authority or superiority over others who disagree with them.

On the other hand, this rhetorical power play can be used to *distance* oneself from others who *claim to be like you,* and maybe even claim authority over you. It is clear why Christians or Muslims might want to use this tactic when talking about the Crusades or Al-Qaeda. By claiming that the Crusaders were not really Christian or that Al-Qaeda is not really Muslim, they get to distance themselves from those other groups. If I say "they are not really scholars"—simultaneously implying that I *am* a true scholar—I am actually saying something like this: "I call myself a scholar and they call themselves scholars, but I'm not like them!" In one of his essays, Bruce Lincoln offers a definition of what historians of religion should do, and says that anyone who falls outside that definition should not be identified as a historian, and then sarcastically adds that they might rightly be called a "cheerleader, voyeur, [or] retailer of import goods" (Lincoln 1996, 227). The implication is clear: "cheering on religion and writing a history of religion are not the same—do not confuse what I do with what cheerleaders do."

Certainly, this is to some extent understandable—people who self-identify as Muslim are usually very different from one another in many respects. Identifying someone as a Muslim does not tell us very much about her—she could be conservative or progressive; she could be sexist or a feminist; she could be for an Islamic state or against an Islamic state—and she could define what that means in any of a thousand different ways.

Identifying someone as a Christian may not tell us much about her, either—she may or may not believe in the trinity; she may or may not go to church every Sunday (or every day, for that matter); she may or may not believe in the separation of church and state. She *probably* believes in God and Jesus, but even that can probably get us in trouble—think about the "death of God" theologians mentioned above, who believed that the authority of God was an obstacle to realizing the love of Christ. We make a mistake when we lump together all who identify as Christian or all who identify as Muslim, as if they all shared the same views or practices. It's a popular mistake, but a mistake nonetheless.

So this strategy of talking about "real Christianity" is a handy rhetorical device for separating yourself from others, or for claiming that your own views or practices are superior to those of others. But how could we decide between competing authenticity claims? The crusaders certainly considered themselves true Christians, and those who are called Muslim extremists certainly view themselves as true Muslims. Is it really true that those Christians who led the Crusades were *not really* Christians? Is it really true, as some Muslims claim, that "fundamentalist Islam" is *not really* Islam?

Defining Authentic Christianity: Mission Impossible

The Ontario Consultants on Religious Tolerance host a website called religioustolerance.org. On one of their pages, they consider what methods one might use to find out which religion is the "true" religion. One possible method is to "pray to God and ask to be enlightened." Apart from the fact that it is unclear *which* god one would pray to, they note "*This method appears to be unreliable.* When people pray to God for enlightenment, most seem to conclude that *their own* religion and faith group is the true one" (www.religioustolerance.org/reltrue.htm; emphasis added). When people use the tools of their own religious tradition for answers, they typically end up validating their own tradition. There seem to be no reliable ways to decide between different claims about who does or does not have the true form of a religion. Every group brings its own set of priorities and values to a religion, and in the process remakes that religion, ever so subtly, for themselves.

Let's look at an important example: the beginning of "orthodoxy" in the early Christian community. A review of the writings of early Christians shows that there were *many different groups* who considered themselves followers of Jesus in the first few centuries, and they generally had *very different ideas* about who Jesus was and why he was significant. It is for this reason that scholars sometimes talk about early "Christianities" in the plural, rather than just early "Christianity." There does not seem to have been one "true" Christianity since the beginning; all the evidence points to the fact that there were *always* several branches of Christianity.

Elaine Pagels outlines the wide variety of forms of early Christianity in *The Gnostic Gospels*. Pagels demonstrates that some early Christians believed that Jesus literally rose from the dead, but other Christians thought that the idea was "extremely revolting, repugnant, and impossible"—these Christians apparently believed that a symbolic interpretation of the "resurrection" was far superior to the idea of a zombie-Jesus coming back from the dead (Pagels 1979, 5). Some early Christians believed that there was one god and only one god, but other Christians believed this to be patent nonsense—for the latter group it appeared obvious that although there might be a supreme god, there were other "demigods" (or smaller gods) out there as well (Pagels 1979, 44). Some early Christians believe that God the Father and Jesus the Son were male, but that the Holy Spirit was neutral, whereas other early Christians believed that the Holy Spirit was female or a "mother" (Pagels 1979, 62ff). Some early Christians claimed that Jesus literally suffered and died on the cross before rising from the dead, but other Christians insisted that Jesus was a spiritual being incapable of suffering or dying, and only *appeared* to have suffered and died on the cross (Pagels 1979,

87ff). This one book provides us with quite a few examples, but there are many more to be found in history. In sum, *there were many forms of Christianity from the very beginning.*

Why did these different groups not just use the Bible to sort out who was right and who was wrong? Simple: because *there was no Bible.* The early Christians had hundreds of stories (some spread by word of mouth and some written down), collections of sayings, letters, testimonies, prophecies, and other documents that were circulating throughout their communities in the Roman Empire. Today they are easy to find, although in the past many of them had been suppressed. A good collection of primary sources from early Christianity (such as Bart Ehrman's *After the New Testament*) will include, for instance:

- The Gospel According to the Ebionites,
- The Secret Book of John,
- The Gospel of Truth,
- The Wisdom of Jesus Christ,
- The Gospel of Phillip,
- The Gospel of Thomas,
- The Gospel of Peter,
- The Proto-Gospel of James,
- The Infancy Gospel of Thomas.

Some of these texts were lost (or suppressed) for some time, but recovered at a later time. The study of these books reveals themes and narratives that have completely reshaped how scholars think about the early Christian church. Although much of their content is the same as or similar to what we find in the New Testament gospels, some of it is considerably unique. In the Infancy Gospel of Thomas there is a story about how Jesus as a toddler murdered a boy who stumbled into him by accident: "a child who was running banged into his shoulder. Jesus was angered and said to him, 'You shall go no further on your way.' And immediately the child fell down dead" (Ehrman 1999b, 256). When Joseph (his father) confronts him, Jesus says: "You have acted very stupidly. … Do not vex me" (Ehrman 1999b, 256). In the Gospel of Peter, Jesus appears as a giant after he rose from the dead, being carried by two other giants: "[The soldiers] then saw three men exit the tomb; two supported the one, and a cross followed them. The heads of the two reached up to the heaven, but the one they supported with their hands stretched beyond the heavens" (Ehrman 1999b, 246). Other weird things happen; for example, the cross starts talking to the soldiers. In the Gospel of Thomas, Jesus says that he will turn Mary—it's unclear which Mary he's talking about—into a man: "I shall guide her so that I will make her male, in order that she also may become a living spirit, being like you males. For everyone woman who makes herself male will enter the Kingdom of Heaven" (Ehrman 1999b, 244).

Of course, the fact that there were lots and lots of Christian texts circulating created conflicts between different groups, especially when they disagreed about which ones should be regarded as the most authoritative texts. This conflict was brought to a head when an early Christian leader named Marcion established a specific set of documents as authoritative: he rejected most of the documents circulating at the time, and created the first official Bible. Marcion included in his Bible an edited version of the Gospel of Luke and ten letters attributed to the apostle Paul, but rejected all of the other texts that were available to him—including all of the Jewish Scriptures, which Christians called the Old Testament. Marcion insisted that Jesus' god was not the same god described in the Old Testament—that god was just a demigod—and that the Old Testament was so different from the teachings of Jesus that they could not be reconciled. It is not that he did not believe in the god of the Old Testament, or even that the god of the Old Testament created the world. On the contrary, the fact that the god of the Old Testament created the world was a mark against him: "Why, [Marcion] asked, would a God who is 'almighty'—all powerful—create a world that includes suffering, pain, disease—even mosquitos and scorpions? Marcion concluded that these must be different Gods" (Pagels 1979, 33).

This was not well received by many of Marcion's contemporaries. The early church father Irenaeus of Lyons stated in no uncertain terms that Marcion and those like him "cause the death of many, through the good name [of Jesus] spreading their evil doctrine, and through the gentleness and mercy of this name presenting the bitter and malignant poison of the serpent" (Grant 1997, 96). Out of their shared hatred of Marcion, a coalition of other Christians mounted an attack and created their own Bible. One of the earliest lists of authoritative texts—which dates to the second century, probably not long after Marcion—is called the "Muratorian Canon." Irenaeus himself (in the second century) and Origen (in the third) each had their own canons. According to the historian Eusebius, who wrote in the fourth century, the people of his own day were still debating which texts to include. Eventually a consensus was formed among the Christians, and Marcion lost—in part because the dominant coalition was better at enlisting the support of the emperors—so that the "standard" Christian canon, or set of authoritative documents considered exclusively as "scripture," was finally established. This standard canon included a lot of writings that Marcion rejected, including the Old Testament, four gospels, Paul's letters, several other letters (such as those attributed to James and to Peter), and a few odds and ends (such as Revelation). However, even this collection of scriptures wasn't entirely stable. When the Protestant Reformation happened, many Protestants rejected some of the Old Testament that the Catholics had held as authoritative for centuries. Martin Luther wanted to throw out even more, such as the Epistle of James; but this was too controversial and he had to relent.

In summary, there have been many different groups throughout history that call themselves "Christian," and many of them have had a different Bible. Is there an objective way to determine whether Marcion's or the Roman Catholic Church's or Luther's Bible is the authentic one? How could we justify saying one group was right and the others are wrong? Who is to say that Marcion's form of Christianity, now forgotten, was not "the real" Christianity?

Defining Authentic Hinduism: Mission Impossible

We encounter the same problems when it comes to definitions of "authentic" Hinduism as we found with Christianity. In *Rethinking Hindu Identity*, D.N. Jha shows how most modern definitions of Hinduism suffer from serious problems.

First, some Hindu thinkers point to the subcontinent of India as the basis for Hindu identity. On this view, "Bharata"—the native name for India—grounds Hindu identity just as some Israelites view Israel as the basis of their identity. The people from Bharata are the ones who rightly bear a Hindu identity. This view is built in part on a narrative of a golden age of Indian or Hindu culture:

> In this ... format India, i.e., Bharata, is timeless. The first man was born here. Its people were the authors of the first human

> civilization, the Vedic [civilization] … The authors of this civilization had reached the highest peak of achievement in all arts and sciences, and they were conscious of belonging to the Indian nation, which has existed eternally. (Jha 2009, 10)

This view is linked to the modern Hindu nationalist movement; the agenda of this movement involves—in part—expelling Muslims from India because their race and culture is understood not to have come from ancient Bharata. If "we" have our origins in ancient Bharata, but "they" have their origins elsewhere, then they don't belong in India. As Jha points out, this view "legitimates the … perception of national identity as located in remote antiquity, accords centrality to the supposed primordiality to Hinduism and thus spawns Hindu cultural nationalism" (Jha 2009, 14).

The problem with this view, however, is that the existence of an eternal and unchanging Bharata is a fiction. Jha demonstrates that the borders or boundaries of Bharata changed throughout time, as is evident upon consideration of ancient Indian texts. Just as the boundaries of the original thirteen colonies of the United States have expanded, retreated, and expanded over time, so did "Bharata" move—there is no one location that always was and is Bharata. In addition, the archaeological evidence found in various places across India demonstrates that there was not a unified, unchanging Indian culture across Bharata (see Jha 2009, 14). So the basis of Hindu identity in the land will not work.

A second way of defining Hindu identity is linked specifically to the use of the term "Hindu" by people who wrote about ancient India; the claim is that ancient people identified Indian religion as the "Hindu" religion. Perhaps Hindu identity is linked not to the land but to an ancient religious culture. The problem is that ancient people did not appear to have used the word "Hindu" to refer to a religious culture. On the contrary, the word tended to be used in a way that had a "geographic, linguistic, or ethnic connotation" (Jha 2009, 15). That is, when the word "Hindu" was used, people were sometimes referring to a location, a language, or a racial or ethnic group: "The term 'Hindu' continued to have several meanings in subsequent times" (Jha 2009, 15). In addition, Jha (2009, 17) notes this is further complicated by the fact that Indians themselves did not "describe themselves as Hindus before the fourteenth century"—that is, not only did outsiders not refer to a "Hindu religion" in ancient India, but Indians themselves did not use the term *at all* before the fourteenth century. The idea that there has been an eternal, unchanging, and obviously identifiable "Hindu" religious identity from the beginning of Indian civilization turns out to be nonsense. On the contrary, the characterization of ancient Indian culture as being part of the "Hindu religion" is demonstrably anachronistic.

A third way of defining Hindu identity has been based around the Vedas, ancient Indian texts that are sometimes thought to serve as a "foundation" for Hinduism, just as the Bible is assumed to serve as a "foundation" for Judaism or Christianity. Some "scholars of religion … define Hinduism as 'the religion of those humans who create, perpetuate, and transform traditions with legitimizing reference to the authority of the Vedas'" (Jha 2009, 21, quoting Smith 1989, 13–14). Those who take this approach "referred nostalgically to the earliest period of Indian past as one of 'Vedic harmony'—a period where people were 'ruled according to the principles of the Vedas and India enjoyed 2000 years of uninterrupted peace, tranquility and prosperity'" (Jha 2009, 2, quoting Misra 2004, 37). However, grouping together Hindus on the basis of adherence to the Vedas won't work either, simply because there is historical evidence that the Vedas were often authoritative in word but not deed, and sometimes not even in word—the idea that the Vedas have been authoritative for all who self-identify as Hindu is fictional (Jha 2009, 21). Later "Hindu" texts supposedly based on the Vedic tradition, such as the Upanishads and the Bhagavad Gita, actually *criticize* the Vedas. The historical evidence demonstrates that so-called Hindu "sects have not had the same attitude toward the Vedic corpus, and even the texts of specific sectarian affiliations often express contradictory views about it" (Jha 2009, 25).

The historical and archaeological evidence shows that there have been a wide variety of racial, ethnic, and cultural groups in India, and there are no commonalities to be found among them all. Why posit a unified identity where none exists? Jha (2009, 3) makes it clear why Indians might have invented the fiction of an eternal unchanging "Hindu" identity. "The demonization of Muslims was a prominent theme" in the nineteenth-century literature on Hindu identity. The rise in importance of "Hindu" identity in this literature was clearly linked to anti-Islamic sentiment: many Indians who wanted to expel Muslims from the country argued for expulsion on the basis of the claim that Muslims were infiltrating and infecting the purity of India or Hinduism. If Muslims did not descend from the original ancestors of Bharata, if they were not identified as "Hindu," or if they were not practicing the original religion of the Vedas, then they did not belong in India. In the end, the fabrication of a timeless Hindu identity appears to have been a power play born out of racial, ethnic, and cultural hatred of some Indians toward Muslims in their midst.

Authenticity and Essentialism

The issue here is the problem of essentialism. The search for a "true Christianity" or a "true Hinduism" behind the label is a fool's errand; if we look for the essence we are going to be looking forever. As we noted in Chapter 2, in place of essences what we inevitably find is that categories (1) group together dissimilar things, (2) identify things that are constantly shifting and changing, and (3) identify things that are not really "things" so much as sets of relationships.

First, there is no one "thing" called Christianity because the term collects together a lot of different groups of people that do not have one set of things in common. Any review of the historical record proves this to be the case.

Second, there is no one thing called Christianity because those things that fall under the category are constantly evolving and changing. "You cannot step in the same river twice" applies to Christianity too—Christianity today has shifted, swirled, and changed from what it was long ago. "Popular cultures and popular religions are not in any way immobile: they undergo evolutions, transformations, and even metamorphoses" (Bayart 2005, 66). Specifically, change over time

> arises because religions, like 'cultures' more broadly, have no essential components that are inherently stable over time: old doctrines are replaced by new ones, existing rituals die out in favor of ritual innovations, and organizational structures are transformed. Innovations arise when the selection of religious elements from the repertoire changes, when existing elements are discarded or new elements are introduced. (Hammer 2009, 11)

That is, change over time takes place because the tools in the cultural toolbox are discarded, rearranged, or replaced by new tools. None of these tools are essential, and no single tool is used in identical ways over time, in which case no "essence" to Christianity among the various tools (and their uses) can be found:

> For many, religion is a "given," with religions such as Christianity and Islam often being viewed as static [or] eternal .... In practice, however, religious organisations and religious cultures are as subject to change and influence as any other human activity. (Nye 2008, 52)

Last, there is no one "thing" called Christianity because it is not a "thing," but a set of relations. For instance, most forms of what falls under the category "Christianity" are made up of (always changing and shifting) relationships between classifications, people, elements of cultural toolboxes, authoritative figures, authoritative texts, legitimating discourses, and so on. If we dig through all these things and look for a solid "essence" underlying all the relations, we are being just as silly as a child looking for calories in a bowl of ice cream. As Tim Murphy rightly suggests, "All identity is … relational: no thing can be abstracted out of a set of relations" (Murphy 2007, 120); and this applies to so-called religious identities as much as any other.

Sometimes it seems that every religious tradition contains much more variety than similarity: many people who call themselves Hindus have different ideas about what makes a Hindu; many people who call themselves Buddhists have different ideas about what makes a Buddhist. At the end of the day, all we have are their stories, their *claims* to authenticity, rather than authenticity itself. We cannot decide who really is or is not a Buddhist or a Hindu—if anyone is at all. Our only option is to ask this question: *why* are these claims being made? Whose authority is supported by claims to authenticity? Who holds power? And who gets to do what to whom?

Where Does This Leave Us?

So what *can* we do? Is it even worth talking about "Christianity", "Hinduism," or "Buddhism," or is it all so relative that there's nothing to even hang words on? What can we do to better understand religion and how it works?

Once, during a class discussion about how identities are assigned by communities, a student asked me whether she was Catholic. She had been baptized, had received first communion, and had been confirmed, but she didn't really believe in any of the Catholic doctrines anymore. Was she still Catholic?

When confronted with a question about who is or isn't authentic, the best strategy is to not address the question directly at all, but to look *behind* the question and ask "Who wants to know, and why do you need to know it?" When we are asking who "is" and "isn't" part of a tradition, we are wrongly searching for an essence we will not find. What we need to look at is not authenticity ("are you authentic?") but *function* ("how does this work?"). What kind of *identification* happens when we use certain words? What are their *effects* of this identification for us and our relationships? Who wants to know? And why?

In "Rites of Institution" (an essay in *Language and Symbolic Power*, 1999), Pierre Bourdieu suggests that identities work *collectively*. An identity does not happen in a vacuum. Hermits do not have substantial identities; only people who are active in groups have identities that help define how others interact with them. For Bourdieu, we use something called "rites of institution" to cause an identity to be *publicly* recognized. For example, when a person is knighted, he is *instituted* as a knight in the eyes of others. When a president is sworn in, she is *instituted* as a president for that country. They are not a knight or a president when they are lost in the wilderness—nor even, necessarily, in a foreign country. For Bourdieu, these identities would not work or would not function if others did not recognize them. A self-proclaimed president has none of the powers of a president if no-one *recognizes* her as president. At one point in the fifteenth century three different people all claimed to be the true pope of the Catholic Church at the same time. However, none of the three could garner everyone's recognition—each one's authority as "pope" extended only as far as he was recognized.

The student's question—"am I Catholic?"—gets at the heart of this entire problem: if she went through the rites of institution, such that she was publicly instituted and publicly recognized as a full member of the Catholic Church, does that mean that she *is* Catholic, even if she does not individually recognize herself as such? Who gets to determine her identity? Does she get to *institute* it herself, or is it instituted for her *by the community*? Is she really Catholic or not?

To address this question, as we said, we need to answer the question *behind* it. The problem is that this kind of question makes us forget that naming or identifying is an action or a process. It is not helpful to think in terms of the verb "to be" here. What we need to do is think of a *verb*, an *action*, or a *process*: "to name," "to label," "to identify." A more useful question than "Is she Catholic?" would be "*Who* identifies her as Catholic?"

Possibly the most important element here is the "who" in "who identifies?" Philosopher Chiara Bottici points out that different persons and different groups will use identities in different ways, and that means that there is no one stable use of an identity. Even within a group of reasonably similar people who all identify one another as Christians, they may use the word "Christian" slightly differently. In addition, their uses of the word "Christian" will probably change over time as the group evolves, and especially as people die and are replaced by new members. "The problem is that there is not a single 'self' that can tell the whole story. … [I]n the case of groups, we do not have just one, but many living bodies with many different stories of recognitions [or identifications] to tell" (Bottici 2007, 241). This is particularly a problem if we are social constructionists. If words make worlds, then groups only exist because they are created by humans. Bottici puts it this way:

> In the case of social entities such as nations, classes and states, we are not dealing simply with abstract notions, but with socially constructed beings: it is because there are narrating bodies [i.e., groups that make identifications] that behave *as if* such beings existed, that they do *actually* exist.
>
> (Bottici 2007, 241; see also Cohen 1985)

However, "in group identities, there is no single narrating body that can tell the whole story"—simply because groups are always divided among themselves and divided from outsiders about how they imagine their group identity—"therefore, it can always be the case that *there is no common story at all*" (Bottici 2007, 244; emphasis added). For Bottici, there can never be one account of a group identity because those identities are created by the way they are imagined by both insiders and outsiders, and not only might insiders and outsiders have different ideas, but, additionally, insiders are almost always divided among themselves. A social fact is still a "fact" as far as it is recognized by a community—but if a community *is split* on their use of an identification, then there are no "facts" to be had about that identity.

Religion scholar Aaron W. Hughes makes the same point in his discussion of how some scholars misguidedly search for an essence to "Islam." Is it essentially peaceful? Is it essentially violent? Hughes argues that these searches are misguided; such an approach cannot provide "a proper understanding of something called Islam precisely because no such thing can exist. Despite appeals to the contrary by either practitioners or scholars of the tradition, Islam, like any other religious tradition, is a series of sites of contestation" (Hughes 2007, 54). That is, there is no "thing" called "Islam," there is just a series of contested and variable claims about what "Islam" is (see also McCutcheon 2005, 47–63). Similarly, Jean-François Bayart says that it is impossible to find essences behind authenticity claims: "Hard as I have looked, so far I have seen only *processes* of forming cultural or political identities" (Bayart 2005, 85; emphasis added). That is, there is no authentic essence to be found, only the *process of people claiming authenticity*. As a result, we cannot study "Islam" itself—since it doesn't exist—although *we can* study all those different groups that make claims about what Islam really is or is not. I would even go so far as Bayart does: to be as precise as possible, we would have to say that "there is no such thing as identity, only operational *acts of identification*" (Bayart 2005, 92; emphasis added).

Replacing the question "Is my student Catholic?" with "Who identifies her as Catholic?" helps us to see that naming or identifying is an action or a process that always takes place between at least four elements. We should not ask "Is she Catholic?" Rather, we should ask (1) *who* is identified by (2) *whom* as (3) *what*, and (4) with what *effects*?

So, in this case, we could say that (1) my *student* is identified by (2) some *Churches* as (3) *Catholic*, and (4) with the effect that she is *entitled to the privileges* associated with that identity, such as the right to take Holy Communion or confess to a priest.

However, we could also say that (1) my *student* is identified by (2) *herself* as (3) *not Catholic*, and (4) with the effect that those people she tells that to will *disassociate* her from the local community that self-identifies as Catholic.

Here's another example. We could say that in 1775—immediately before the American Revolution—(1) *King George* was identified by (2) *the white people living on the east coast of North America* as (3) *king* of their territory, and (4) with the effect that *his decisions were recognized* as authoritative for their community.

We could also say that in 1777—immediately *after* the start of the American Revolution—(1) *King George* was identified by (2) *certain white people living on the east coast of North America* as (3) *not king* of their territory, and (4) with the effect that they *did not recognize his decisions* as authoritative for their community and felt justified in mounting an armed resistance.

We could add that in 1777, (1) *the people living in England* identified (2) *King George* as (3) *king of the white people living on the east coast of North America*, and (4) with the effect that *he was able to mobilize England's army* in an attempt to regain military control of the east coast of North America.

So the question "Was King George *really* the king of America?" is an unhelpful question with no good answer—it would be better to ask *who* identified him as *what* and *who did not*, and *with what effects*.

Another student once told me that he was one-eighth Native American, and asked whether this made him *really* Native American. I asked what box he checked on his college application, and he said that he had checked "Native American" because this made him eligible for additional financial aid. So I told him that (1) *he* was identified (2) by his *college* as (3) *Native American*, and (4) with the effect that he was *eligible for certain financial scholarships*. Of course, in other contexts, particularly public contexts in which Native Americans would suffer discrimination or even be subject to violence, he might serve his own interests by identifying as white instead of Native American. The question "Is he *really* white or *really* Native American?" is not useful. There are no essences to be found, only authenticity claims in process; what matters is not what he "is" but who identifies him as what and with what effects.

Conclusion

What we have argued in this chapter is that the work of sorting out who is *authentically* a member of a group and who is not *cannot be done* because essences do not exist. In addition, authenticity claims usually look a lot like power plays and can be analyzed as such. We should replace questions about *authenticity* with investigations into *the process of identification:* who claims identities for themselves or others, who recognizes those identities, and what consequences, benefits, or penalties follow from that identification. Who wants to know? And why?

Michael Servetus identified himself as a Christian, but John Calvin and the authorities in Geneva did not. The consequence of their refusal to recognize him as Christian was that they were legally permitted to burn him at the stake. Rather than trying to determine who was right and who wasn't right, the more useful questions focus instead on how *power* was able to manifest according to the definitions used. Who wants to know? And why? Who spoke? Who stood up and identified themselves? Who listened? Who benefitted? And who was allowed to do what to whom?

8

Case Study: What Would Jesus Do?

The phrase "What would Jesus do?" became widely popular in the United States in the 1990s among evangelical Christians, who would wear bracelets and related paraphernalia bearing this motto. Interestingly, this is not a new Christian phenomenon: the phrase was first popularized in Charles Sheldon's novel, *In His Steps*, which appeared in 1896 (though I use the 1899 edition). In this novel, a minister challenges the members of his church to join him in a pact of sorts, according to which they will devote themselves for one full year to living as they believe Jesus would. They commit to asking themselves daily what Jesus would do if he were in their situations, and promise to follow through on their answers.

This novel is of interest because in it we can find almost all of the elements we have covered in this book: classification, social stratification, domination, habitus, legitimation, authority, authenticity claims, and so on. In this chapter I will provide a reading of this novel, showing how the method and theory I have proposed can shed light on a specific text.

Charles Sheldon's *In His Steps*

The story takes place in a town called Raymond, somewhere in America's Midwest, and centers around the activities of the members of the First Church of Raymond, a Protestant Christian Church. It begins as the minister at the church, Henry Maxwell, is preparing his Sunday sermon on a passage in the New Testament about following in Jesus' steps. While he is working, a sickly and "shabby-looking young man" characterized as a "tramp" comes to the door, asking for help finding a job (Sheldon 1899, 2). Reverend Maxwell claims he knows of no jobs and quickly dismisses the tramp, returning to his sermon.

During the next Sunday morning's church service, just after Maxwell had completed his sermon, the tramp returns. He interrupts the service as it is closing, walks up the center aisle to the pulpit, and turns around to address the church members. He tells them that he recently lost his job, his wife recently died, and that is daughter is staying with another family until he can find work. However, he implicitly criticizes them for offering him no help, despite their apparent commitment to following in Jesus' steps:

> But I was wondering … if what you call following Jesus is the same thing as what He taught. What did He mean when He said, "Follow me"? The minister said … that it was necessary for the disciple of Jesus to follow His steps, and he said the steps were obedience, faith, love, and imitation. But I did not hear him tell just what he meant that to mean, especially the last step. What do Christians mean by following the steps of Jesus? I've tramped through this city for three days trying to find a job and in all that time I've not had a word of sympathy or comfort except from your minister here, who said he was sorry for me and hoped I would find a job somewhere. … [W]hat I feel puzzled about is, what is meant by following Jesus? Do you mean that you are suffering and denying yourselves and trying to save lost humanity just as I understand Jesus did? … Somehow I get puzzled when I see so many Christians living in luxury and singing, "Jesus, I my cross have taken, all to leave and follow Thee," and remember how my wife died in a tenement in New York City, gasping for air and asking God to take the little girl too. Of course I don't expect you people can prevent every one from dying of starvation, lack of proper nourishment and tenement air, but what does following Jesus mean? (Sheldon 1899, 10–12)

The tramp seems to assume that following Jesus would include, at least in part, helping poor or jobless individuals such as himself. As such, the key to the tramp's speech is his implicit suggestion that these people are claiming to be Christians, claiming to be following in Jesus' steps, but that in reality they are living in luxury while many people outside this church—such as himself—are starving. He implies that they are hypocrites (that is, *inauthentic* Christians). However, in the middle of his comments to the church, he passes out onto the floor. The minister takes him into his house and hires a doctor to look over him, but within the week he dies.

The death of the tramp makes a remarkable impact on Maxwell. The next Sunday he tells his church that "much that the man said was so vitally true" (16), and asks them to volunteer to "pledge themselves earnestly and honestly for an entire year not to do anything without first asking the question, 'What would Jesus do?' And after asking that question, each one will follow Jesus as exactly as he knows how, no matter what the results may be" (17).

About fifty members of the church stay after the service to meet and discuss the pledge (although the number who take the pledge later grows to around one hundred; 98). They begin the meeting with a prayer and then go on to consider how they will go about answering the question, "What would Jesus do?," since the answers may not be obvious. Protestant Christianity was formed in part on the basis of the slogan *sola scriptura*, which means "scripture alone," so it is surprising that their first consideration is, in fact, not to turn to the Bible in order to answer these questions. Instead, Maxwell claims, "There is no way that I know of ... except as we study Jesus through the medium of the Holy Spirit" (20). That is, they decide to *pray* to their god and ask what they call the Holy Spirit to speak to them. The members of the church mention that there is bound to be disagreement—it is unlikely that every member will be in full agreement about what Jesus might do in any particular context or situation. Maxwell agrees, but suggests that their answers will not be too varying: "The standard of Christian action cannot vary in most of our acts" (21). Maxwell goes on to add, however, that they must be "free from fanaticism on one hand and too much caution on the other. If Jesus' example is the example for the world, it certainly must be feasible to follow it" (21–2).

In addition, although they do not say so in this first meeting, it becomes clear throughout the novel that the members of this church are implicitly guided by the ideals of honesty (81, 88) and selflessness, especially the latter. They seem to insist repeatedly throughout the novel that their actions should be guided by the welfare or suffering of others, rather than their own interests. This calls for, in many cases, a great deal of self-sacrifice on their part—and they view the avoidance of self-sacrifice as a terrible sin. At one point Maxwell uses the words "self-denial and suffering" to describe the ideal at which they are aiming (70).

It is worth noting that the interests of others include not only material interests (i.e., the hunger and joblessness of the tramp), but also what they would view as "spiritual" interests (i.e., they are concerned with the salvation of souls through the personal conversion to Christianity, without which they believe an individual will go to hell).

Edward Norman, editor of the local paper, is one of the individuals who enters this pact by taking the pledge. His first response is to take all tobacco and liquor advertisements out of the paper, as he believes that Jesus would not support the sale of these products. In addition, he decides to remove all stories about boxing matches, although it is unclear whether this is due to an objection to boxing itself or the gambling that often goes along with boxing matches. He also removes salacious accounts of local crime, as well as all gossip columns. The Sunday edition of the paper is permanently cancelled, as he believes Jesus would rest rather than work on the Sabbath.

The attempt to run the paper as Jesus might is not well received by others on the paper's staff. His assistant predicts that these changes "will simply ruin the paper. … Why, it isn't feasible to run a paper now-a-days on any such basis" (26). Although Norman is fully willing to face the risks, his assistant's prediction eventually turns out to be right—subscriptions wane and the paper almost goes bankrupt later in the novel.

Alexander Powers, a superintendent at the local railroad machine shop, implements his pledge in two ways. First, he decides to take a store room at the company and convert it into a break room for the laborers:

> I am going to fit it up with tables and a coffee plant in the corner … My plan is to provide a good place where the men can come and eat their noon lunch and give them, two or three times a week, the privilege of a fifteen minutes' talk on some subject that will be a real help to them in their lives. (44–5)

What Powers means is that he intends to invite Reverend Maxwell to give mini-sermons to the laborers during their lunch break in the room

Powers has provided them. The second way of implementing his pledge involves tattling on his company for illegal activity. What happens is that an envelope containing information related to his company's illegal business was accidentally put in Powers' mailbox at work, and he opens it before noticing that it was not addressed to him. He discovers his company's violation of a number of "Interstate Commerce Laws" (47), and decides that what Jesus would do would be to report the violations to the government. Powers does so, simultaneously resigning from his position at the railroad machine shop. For Sheldon, this appears to be a perfect example of self-sacrifice in the name of honesty.

Rachel Winslow, a young woman with an apparently amazing voice, is slow to decide what Jesus would do in her situation. At first she is made an offer from a traveling opera company, which, although it would have made her wealthy and famous, she turns down because accepting the offer would have made a selfish rather than selfless use of her singing talents. She explicitly states, "I am completely convinced ... that Jesus would never use any talent like a good voice just to make money" (51). She's not quite sure what she wants to do with her talent, but in the short term she decides she will help out with some local revival meetings.

The revival meetings are led by Mr and Mrs Gray, who have set up a tent for Christian services in a section of Raymond called "the Rectangle" (these are referred to as the White Cross tent meetings in the novel, although it is unclear where the name "White Cross" comes from). The Rectangle is a part of town near many of the factories and machine shops, and where a number of bars and pubs can be found. Though it is never explicitly said, readers get the impression that many laborers leave work at the factories and shops and head directly to the bars in the Rectangle. Since the characters see these patrons of bars as unsaved—and therefore going to hell—they find the Rectangle to be the perfect place to hold the tent services. As Rachel puts it, "It is in a part of the city where Christian work is most needed" (65). Therefore Rachel lends her talent to the Grays, and according to the narrator, her voice brings drunks out of the bars and into the tent meeting much like sirens draw sailors to their deaths: "Several windows near by went up. Some men quarreling in a saloon stopped and listened. Other figures were walking rapidly in the direction of the Rectangle and the tent" (68). Because of her talent, the tent quickly filled up and began "to run over" (69).

Virginia Page is an heiress sitting on a million dollars (which was an exorbitant amount of money in the 1890s). She has to decide what Jesus might do with the money she's inherited, but of course has difficulty: since Jesus was relatively impoverished according to the New Testament, there is no model as such provided for what he might do with wealth. "There could be no one, fixed, Christian way of using money. The rule that regulated its use was unselfish utility" (109). She eventually decides to use half of her money to endow Norman's newspaper, in order to prevent it from sliding into bankruptcy as he turns it into a "Christian" newspaper (127). The other half of her money she decides she will put to use by building some sort of lodging houses or schools for women in the Rectangle, and she intends to partner with Rachel in order to provide these women with a music program of some sort (146–8).

By contrast, Madam Page—Virginia's grandmother—will have nothing to do with the "What would Jesus do?" pledge. She is described as a woman of "wealth and social standing" (53), and it seems to follow that she is more concerned with her reputation among her peers than her Christian faith. In fact, she practically insults Rachel, explicitly describing the pact as "foolish," "impossible," and rooted in "false emotion" (57): "I felt confident at the time that those who promised [to take the pledge] would find out after a trial and abandon it as visionary and absurd" (56).

Virginia's response to her grandmother's challenge is put thus: "Do you mean ... that we cannot possibly act as Jesus would, or do you mean that if we try to, we shall offend the customs and prejudices of society?" (57). Virginia implicitly makes a distinction between two choices: one can follow Jesus or one can follow society; she makes it clear that her grandmother is selfishly choosing society over Jesus. Madam Page is unmoved; she responds with condescension, and suggests that Rachel will see the truth of the matter soon enough.

Another member of the pact is Milton Wright, a man who owns a number of stores. Prior to making the pledge he was the sort of man who ran his business "from the standpoint of 'Will it pay?,'" but subsequent to the pledge he is "compelled to revolutionize the whole method of business" (85–6). He sets aside profit as a goal of his business, and decides that any money he makes will be put to use "for the good of humanity" (87). In addition, he decides that he will view his employees as "souls to be saved" (87).

The plot of the novel develops at first as a series of vignettes focusing on these individuals (and a few others), but later the storyline coalesces around a group effort. Maxwell decides that they should join forces in order to end the licensing of alcohol sales in their town (or, as they refer to it, "license"). Indeed, "[t]he destruction of the saloon is *the* theme of *In His Steps*" (Boyer 1971, 65; emphasis original). Not surprisingly, they see the Rectangle at the center of their efforts. Maxwell's concern about the saloons—a concern he sees as guided by the Holy Spirit—leads him to preach "against the saloon" one Sunday morning. The sermon is timed in relation to upcoming town elections:

> The regular election of city officers was near at hand. The question of license would be an issue in that election. … Was not the most Christian thing they could do to act as citizens in the matter, fight the saloon at the polls, elect good men to city offices, and clean the municipality? (Sheldon 1899, 100–1)

Maxwell's sermon serves to ignite the fervor of those who had made the pact, and the "tension" in the group reaches its "highest point" (101). Following the sermon, Donald Marsh—the president of a local college—talks to Maxwell and they decide to publicly campaign as a team against license for the upcoming election. They enlist Edward Norman, of course, who supports the movement against license in his newspaper.

Around the time that the group campaign against license begins, Virginia takes a special interest in a "homeless, wretched creature" (118) at the Rectangle named Loreen. Virginia's carriage is on its way to the tent meeting at the Rectangle when Loreen, drunk, comes reeling out of a saloon. Loreen had previously converted at the tent meetings, but apparently had reverted to her old ways. Virginia decides to take Loreen, in her drunken stupor, back to her own house in order to take care of her there. Virginia's house, of course, is also Madam Page's house, and Madam Page vehemently opposes this plan of action—not because it was against her faith, but because it was against "her social code of conduct" to bring into her home "the scum of the streets" (120). Virginia, however, stands up to her grandmother: "we call ourselves Christians. Here is a poor, lost human creature, without a home slipping into possible eternal loss, and we have more than enough. I have brought her here and shall keep her" (120). In addition, Virginia rejects

Madam Page's concern with her social reputation: "Society is not my God. … I do not count the verdict of society as of any value" (121).

The first half of the novel (the book can easily be divided into two parts, each part having a relatively self-contained plotline) comes to a climax on the day of the elections. The narrator of the story claims that the Rectangle "boiled and heaved and cursed and turned its worst side out to the gaze of the city" (131). At the same time, an intense tent meeting was held that went on for hours. As they exit the tent, around ten in the evening, the Rectangle appears to be rioting. A rumor has been circulating that license had been defeated in the election—which later turns out to be false (137–8)—and Maxwell and Marsh are attacked by the crowd, which begins throwing stones, mud, and other "missiles" (135). As Maxwell and Marsh make their way through the crowd—followed by Virginia, Rachel, and Loreen—the Rectangle becomes "drunk and enraged" (135). From a saloon window a "heavy bottle" is thrown that hits Loreen, who immediately collapses (135). In seconds she dies, "and the next moment her soul was in Paradise" (136). The narrator notes, however, that "this is only one woman out of thousands killed by this drink devil" (136).

The church members respond by indirectly blaming themselves for her death. They believe themselves to be responsible because if they had opposed license at an earlier point her death could have been prevented. However, "the Christian conscience had been aroused too late" (139). Nevertheless, these sentiments of guilt serve to spur the community to redouble their efforts against license and the saloons, despite their loss in the elections.

The plotline of the novel lacks obvious direction and is a bit rambling, so this place is as good as any to halt summary and begin an analysis.

Analysis: Class and Habitus

Before beginning an analysis I should point out that while we can never know for certain what a person's intentions are, based on what we know of Sheldon's biography—he was a minister of a church and his stated views were similar to those of the characters in the novel—we can assume that Sheldon probably intended for the central characters to be read as exemplary; that is, it is unlikely that he is satirizing late nineteenth-century Christian social movements or anything like that. We can reasonably assume that Sheldon speaks through the voice of the narrator and the voice of some of the "heroes" in the plot, including Reverend Maxwell and Edward Norman.

When this novel first appeared, American society in general was primarily organized not by any Christian categories but by capitalist ones, and therefore it is no surprise that those capitalist categories appear in the novel. There is a clear divide between the *labor class* and the *professional class*. For instance, Marsh explicitly uses the phrase "a class of professional men" (Sheldon 1899, 103) to describe the class to which he and Maxwell belong. Maxwell explicitly uses the language of class when he goes to preach mini-sermons to the laborers at the railroad machine shops during their lunch break. First, he thinks of them as "working men" (45, 46), and notes that he is actually *afraid* to speak to them because of their difference from him. "He actually felt afraid of facing these men ..., [who were] so different from a Sunday audience he was familiar with" (45). When Powers introduced Maxwell to the workers, he "spoke very simply, like one who understands thoroughly the character of his audience" (46). This comment should remind us of Bourdieu's critique of capitalist ideology: "The poor are not just immoral, alcoholic and degenerate, they are stupid, they lack intelligence" (Bourdieu 1998, 43). Sheldon is presenting the members of the working class not only as different, but as possibly intellectually inferior; as Bourdieu rightly insists, this offers members of wealthier classes a reassuring sense of superiority.

Sheldon goes on to differentiate Maxwell further from these laborers: "Like hundreds of other ministers he had never spoken to any gathering except those made up of people of *his own class* in the sense that they were familiar, in their *dress and education and habits*, to him" (Sheldon 1899, 46; emphasis added). Sheldon is describing, without using Bourdieu's vocabulary, this class' *habitus*. They dress differently from Maxwell, they have a different educational level, and they have different *habits*—the last term is, obviously, the root of the word "habitus." Sheldon goes on:

> [Maxwell] had the good sense on this his first appearance not to recognize the men as a class distinct from himself. He did not use the term 'working men,' and did not say a word to suggest any difference between their lives and his own. (46)

That is, their lives *are most definitely different* from his own—he even calls them "a class distinct"—but he had the "good sense" not to draw attention to this fact.

One key element of habitus is language, diction, or way of speaking. This is another way that Sheldon separates out the wealthier classes from the working class. Throughout the novel the people from the church or from Maxwell's class do not speak with an accent of any sort, but the laborers or the characters from the Rectangle almost always do. At one point some characters in the Rectangle say things such as "Who's de bloke?" and "De Fust Church parson," while a drunken man says "Trow out de life line 'cross de dark wave!" (74) These people are members of "a class distinct" or an alternative habitus not only because of their jobs (as working men), their dress, their education, their "habits," but also their manner of speaking.

What sets this class apart from Maxwell's class more than anything else, however, is apparently the consumption of alcohol in the saloons at the Rectangle. The Rectangle, for Sheldon, is tantamount to hell. When Loreen stumbles out of a bar to be picked up by Virginia, they have an interesting exchange of words. When Virginia first grabs her, Loreen screams at her: "You shall not touch me! Leave me! Let me go to hell! That's where I belong! The devil is waiting for me. See him!" (116). At that point Loreen points to the bartender in the saloon she just exited. Of course, Virginia persuades Loreen to come with her, but it is clear that the saloons and the Rectangle are to be understood as hell on earth.

Sheldon uses startling rhetoric to separate the working class who patronize the saloons from the wealthy Christians. Consider the vocabulary Sheldon uses to make up chains of associations (Table 8.1). Sheldon himself, through the voice of the narrator, implies a cosmic dualism: "The end of the week found the Rectangle struggling hard between *two mighty opposing forces*. The Holy Spirit was battling with all His supernatural strength against the saloon devil which had so long held a jealous grasp on its slaves" (emphasis mine; 110). Or: "The Holy Spirit and the Satan of rum seemed to rouse up to a desperate conflict" (132). For Sheldon, one class is literally divine and the other class is literally evil and demonic. Sheldon is, in fact, *literally demonizing* the working class. As the narrator notes at one point, "Jesus is the great divider of life. One must walk either parallel with Him or directly across His path" (130). There is no doubt which side of the divide the working

Table 8.1 Charles Sheldon's rhetorical language.

The good side	*The bad side*
"life of purity" (97)	the Rectangle as "festering sore" (77)
"good men" (101, 104)	"the evil" (77)
"a class of professional men" (103)	"drunken, vile, debauched humanity" (97)
"clean city life" (105)	saloon as "an enemy, not only to the poor and tempted, but ... to the church itself" (100)
"professional men" (105)	"hell of drink" (101)
"organized righteousness" (106)	saloons as "crime-and-shame-producing institutions" (101)
"best men" (107)	city officials who support license are "a corrupt, unprincipled set of men, controlled in large part by the whisky element, and thoroughly selfish" (103)
"decent citizens" (107)	"horrible whirlpool of deceit, bribery, political trickery, and saloonism" (104)
"clean, honest, capable, business-like" (107)	"slums" (105)
"noble" (107)	"whisky-ridden city" (105)
"good citizens" (107)	"rum and corruption" (105)
"cleansing our city" (107)	"cowardly and easily frightened" (106)
"purify our civic life" (107)	"whiskey men" (107)
"lovers of right, purity, temperance, and home" (107)	"corrupt city government" (107)
"long needed reform" (107)	"rule of rum" (107)
"civic righteousness" (108)	"shameless incompetency" (107)
"lovers of Jesus" (109)	"worst enemy known to municipal honesty" (107)
"good" (155)	"evil forces" (108)
	"coarse, brutal, sottish lives" (109)
	"saloon devil" (110)
	"slaves" (110)
	"horror" (110)
	"poor creatures" (110)
	"devilish drink" (110)
	"greatest form of slavery now known to America" (110)
	"whisky forces" (111)
	"aggressive" (111)
	"hatred" (111)
	the saloon as a "deadly viper, hissing and coiling, ready to strike its poison" (111)
	"earthly hell called the saloon" (116)
	the saloon as "enemy of the human race" (154)
	"bad" (155)
	"vileness" (157)
	"the devil" (157)

Numbers in parentheses specify the page(s) on which each description appears Sheldon (1899).

class falls on. To put it in Bourdieu's terms, this absolute distinction between classes seems to be a key feature of the matrix of perception of Sheldon's class—he views the world through this binary distinction.

One commentator suggests:

> In broad outline, we are confronted with an urban 'WASP' [white Anglo-Saxon Protestant] middle class—professional men, managers and minor entrepreneurs, together with their comfortable wives and daughters—which finds itself deeply fearful of, yet simultaneously fascinated by, the burgeoning immigrant working-class population which is crowding into the cities. (Boyer 1971, 67)

In addition, as Bourdieu's account of habitus notes, those who share a habitus will see those with an alternative habitus not only as different—and possibly as something to be afraid of—but as lacking reason, common sense, or even as vulgar or bad. This is borne out in Sheldon's novel. We can see from the list of associations in Table 8.1 that the working class is not only *different* from the wealthy Christians, but also evil, debauched, shameful, coarse, brutal, sottish, vile, and—in short—bad.

This dualism is complicated by the fact that for Sheldon's form of Christianity, the goal is not to discriminate against the working class but to convert them to Christianity. That is, presumably Sheldon wants his intended audience—other Christians—to reach out to those on the wrong side of this class divide and to help bring them over from the dark side. (The language of "good side" and "dark side" may seem unscholarly, but this is exactly the sort of language Sheldon uses; see, for example, his metaphorical use of the language of "darkness" on page 161). However, Sheldon makes it clear that coming over to the good side is incompatible with the habits of the dark side. For instance, when Loreen, after having been saved, reverts to visiting the saloons, Virginia's thoughts were as follows: "She simply saw a soul that had tasted of the joy of a better life slipping back again into its old hell of shame and death" (115). It appears that any alcohol consumption is necessarily on the dark side, and—as Jesus is the great divider—one must choose a side; one cannot both be Christian *and* drink.

On the other hand, being within the wealthy class is not in and of itself redeeming. Madam Page stands out as the paradigmatic hypocrite, as she chooses the standards of society and her reputation among the same over the standards of the church. Maxwell identifies these hypocrites and targets them in a to-do list he makes for himself: "2. Preach fearlessly to the hypocrites in the church no matter what their social importance or wealth" (70). However, this group of hypocrites is still "in the church," still shares his habitus, and can be separated out from the "sinful people in the Rectangle," which he targets in an altogether separate item on his to-do list (70).

In summary, Sheldon's matrix of perception seems to involve a threefold classification for his society:

1 The authentic members of his church and class who make the "What would Jesus do?" pledge.
2 The inauthentic members of his church and class who hypocritically refuse to make the pledge.

---

3 The working class ("a class distinct") who patronize the saloons at the Rectangle.

The gap between his class and the working class appears to be much greater than the gap between those who made the pledge and the hypocrites: the hypocrites are subjected to substantial criticism, but never the demonizing invective directed at the third group. If the hypocrites were really on the wrong side of the line above—that is, if they were considered as demonic as the working class men who drink at the Rectangle—then we would see efforts on the part of the members of the pact to reach out to them. However, we do not. When Powers sets up a space for Maxwell to preach to the people at the railroad, it is *only for* the working class, not for the other members of management—apparently the other members of management, insofar as they share Maxwell and Powers' class, need not be subjected to evangelism. Similarly, Rachel's and Virginia's efforts at the Rectangle are directed solely at the working class and homeless members of the Rectangle. Sheldon seems to be focused narrowly on class difference above all other differences, which contributes to the demonization of the working class alone. While one might think that the difference between "true Christian" and "non-Christian" (as Sheldon defines these) might be central, instead the central difference relevant to the novel is economic class.

Would Sheldon's novel have reinforced or challenged the status quo in 1896? I think any rigorous answer to this will necessarily be divided. On the one hand, Sheldon seems to *intend* to challenge the status quo. The sale of alcohol was clearly legal in most parts of the United States at that time, and Sheldon's novel is aimed at encouraging hypocritical Christians who support license (or who indirectly support it by failing to challenge it) to change their behavior on this issue (we will say more on this below). However, on the other hand, Sheldon's novel not only reflects the class divisions of late nineteenth-century capitalism but seems to teach readers that the division is one with a cosmological significance. That is, many of Sheldon's readers doubtlessly came away with the impression that the class distinction is not unique to capitalism, but runs throughout time and the universe: it is not a *capitalist* distinction—it is perhaps the very distinction between good and evil.

The readers of Maxwell's class who are persuaded by Sheldon's novel learn that the members of a class distinct from their own are not only different, but evil. As we saw above, according to Bourdieu,

> habitus are also classificatory schemes, principles of classification, principles of vision and division, different tastes. They make distinctions between what is good and what is bad, between what is right and what is wrong, between what is distinguished and what is vulgar, and so forth, but the divisions [from one habitus to the next] are not identical. Thus, for instance, the same behavior or even the same good can appear distinguished to one person, pretentious to someone else, and cheap or showy to yet another. (Bourdieu 1998, 8)

What results from this sorting out of society into good and bad classes? Groups will award privileges to members of their own class and will discriminate against those of another class, who they may see as lacking reason or common sense, or who they may see as merely stupid. Because of this, class hierarchies can be reproduced automatically and without people intending them to be reproduced. A system of class habitus can reinforce the status quo in much the same way that a cultural toolbox can legitimate the status quo. It was for this reason that Bourdieu saw that "meritocracy" is a myth—people may "get ahead" in life because of their habitus more than because of their intelligence, effort, or work habits. One's habitus can count as "meritorious," independently of one's ability.

In fact, this is *exactly* the lesson that Sheldon's novel teaches. There is a great deal of collusion between the members of the wealthier class. Fred Morris was a newspaper reporter who took the "What would Jesus do?" pledge, although he worked for a newspaper other than Edward Norman's. When he decided that Jesus wouldn't work on Sundays, he was fired from his job at the other paper. However, because of his connections through his class and his church, Maxwell introduces him to Norman, who offers him a job on the spot. What is interesting is that Norman offers him the job prior to learning anything of Fred's merits, *other than his Christian identity*:

> I can give you a place … I want reporters who won't work Sundays. And what is more, I am making plans for a special kind of reporting which I believe young Morris can develop because he is in sympathy with what Jesus would do.
> (Sheldon 1899, 85)

It is fascinating that the language of "sympathy" is exactly the language Bourdieu used: "[One's] social sense is guided by the system of … signs of which each body is the bearer—clothing, pronunciation, bearing, posture, manners—and which, unconsciously registered, are the basis of 'antipathies' or 'sympathies'" (Bourdieu 1984, 241). For Bourdieu, one's sympathies and antipathies are extended to others on the basis of whether they share one's habitus. It is therefore no surprise to see Norman extending a job to a reporter who shares his way of speaking about Jesus, who shares his habitus, and who therefore shares his sympathies. Later in the novel Norman makes a to-do list similar to Maxwell's: "10. … [Jesus] would probably secure the best and the strongest Christian men and women to cooperate with Him in the matter of contributors [to the paper—i.e., reporters and others writing stories]. That will be my purpose" (Sheldon 1899, 155). As Bourdieu suggests, through the normalization of the dominant habitus, privileges will be extended to individuals who share the dominant habitus, and discrimination will result for those with an alternate habitus. Here Norman explicitly says that he intends to implement a form of religious discrimination in the workplace: he intends to hire people who are Christians like himself. This could not be more clear as an example of collusion. However, there is an element of divine legitimation for this principle of discrimination—it is not only what he intends to do, it is what *Jesus* would probably do.

Bourdieu predicts that, because of the way habitus work, social hierarchies will reproduce themselves over time. It appears that readers persuaded by Sheldon's novel—at least those of Maxwell's class—will learn the lesson that they should extend privileges to those who share their habitus, and discriminate against those with a working class habitus. In addition, the discrimination receives a divine legitimation; those with an alternative habitus are not only seen as bad, vulgar, or stupid (remember: Powers had to speak "simply" to his laborers), as Bourdieu suggests, but also evil, debauched, shameful, coarse, brutal, sottish, and vile (to choose just a few of Sheldon's adjectives). To hire people with such a habitus would doubtlessly be seen as unreasonable, and therefore the gap between the wealthy classes and the working class is likely to be unbreached. Despite Sheldon's apparent intention to encourage those of his class to reach out to those on the dark side, the overall message is that they are not worthy as peers and do not merit jobs until they assimilate to his class's habitus.

To the extent that Sheldon's readers are members of the dominant class—that is, who hold positions of privilege and power—his book and its demonizing message seem more likely to have the effect of widening the class gap than closing it.

> The characters of *In His Steps* are obsessed by thoughts of an immigrant working class of whose existence they are keenly aware, but from whom they feel totally cut off. So deep is this obsession that it generates extreme anxiety at the prospect of actual encounters with the unknown social group. (Boyer 1971, 67)

In fact, the novel probably had the effect of *increasing* that anxiety among its readers. In the end, *In His Steps* offers a divine legitimation of the capitalist class differences of the late nineteenth century; this story about "a class distinct" both reflects and reinforces the social hierarchy.

Analysis: Class Domination

Not only does the novel contribute to the reproduction of a class hierarchy; we can also see how it contributes to class *domination*. Domination, as I have defined it, takes place when classes are set in a relationship that makes it easier for one class to serve its interests than the other. There was clearly a relationship of domination between the wealthier or professional classes and the working class in the late nineteenth century. As we see in the novel, for instance, most of the characters at the church are members of Maxwell's class, and as such have a greater access to capital, privilege, and authority, as well as a greater ability to alter the social arrangements in which they are situated when compared with members of the working class. Edward Norman, Alexander Powers, and Milton Wright have within their power the ability to change the conditions in which they work: Norman completely changes the paper (despite his employees' resistance), Powers has the ability to set up a break room and subject his employees to Maxwell's preaching during lunch, and Wright has the ability to change his company's policies. The laborers who work with them obviously do not have this power, and consequently are subject to a relationship of domination.

In addition, however, and considerably more problematic, is the fact that the habitus of the laborers is counted against them—having a working habitus is tantamount to being stupid (as Powers implies when he speaks "simply" to his workers) or, worse, being demonic. Their access to a position of privilege is prohibited not necessarily because of any *real* lack of merit, but in part simply due to their alternative habitus. Since the requirement that one acclimate to a number of arbitrary social codes is in part what might make one dominated, and since the discrimination on the basis of habitus is, in fact, arbitrary, then this furthers the evidence that the laborers are in a relationship of domination. Since Sheldon's novel reinforces the social hierarchy by recommending on the one hand the extension of unfair privileges to members of the professional class (such as when Norman gives Fred a job simply because he shares the same sympathies or the same habitus) and on the other hand demonizing the working class, this novel can be said to contribute to the reproduction of domination.

What is additionally intriguing about Sheldon's novel is the extent to which it is an exercise in misdirection: the novel seems designed to direct the reader's attention away from the causes of poverty and homelessness of the type seen in the Rectangle (although "designed" here should be subordinated to the "seems" that comes before it—I am sure that no such thing was consciously intended by Sheldon). The actual cause of the tramp's joblessness is very clearly stated in the first chapter of the novel—he lost his job *not* because he was lazy or unproductive (that is, there was no question of his merit), but instead because of the fact that the company he worked for bought machines that made his position redundant:

> I lost my job ten months ago. I am a printer by trade. The new linotype machines are beautiful specimens of invention, but I know six men who have killed themselves inside of the year just on account of those machines. Of course I don't blame the newspapers for getting those machines. Meanwhile, what can a man do? I know I never learned but one trade and that's all I can do. I've tramped all over the country trying to find something. There are a good many others like me. (Sheldon 1899, 10)

The tramp's situation is entirely plausible: these sorts of innovations were widespread during the late nineteenth century, and resulted in a great deal of joblessness for those displaced and low wages for everyone else. "[T]he machine eats work" (Scott 1985, 154).

The problem, of course, was that businesses in competition with one another were in the pursuit of maximum profit. Profits could be raised and prices could be lowered if laborers could be replaced by machines that would perform the same labor more cheaply. However, once one company makes these sorts of changes, others are necessarily quick to follow. This is the nature of market competition: if one company introduces machines and consequently lowers the price of the products they manufacture, they are likely to draw consumers away from other companies. Competing companies are likely to go out of business unless they introduce the same labor-saving devices. Once this cycle starts, a relatively inescapable downward spiral results, where all companies are making the same innovations and laying off laborers.

In addition, once the job market is flooded with laid-off workers, wages go down for workers in general. If there are more jobs than workers, workers can afford to be choosy and negotiate higher salaries; if there are more workers than jobs, workers cannot afford to be choosy and must take whatever they can get. Businesses therefore adjust to the "labor market" and lower the wages offered.

The effects of the combination of the pursuit of profit and market competition are well documented; indeed, it was during the second half of the nineteenth century—at the height of industrialization, but before the rise of substantial laws protecting laborers—that we saw the appearance of extremely exploitative and unsafe labor practices, as well as the wide use of child labor. Karl Marx documented the use of child labor (sometimes starting at even five or six years old), where the children would work fourteen or sixteen hours a day, in working conditions that were literally deadly (often because of poisons or toxins the children were working with; Marx 1990). This sort of exploitative domination resulted directly from the form of market capitalism regnant at the time (these effects of market competition—in particular how they lead to the "squeezing" of labor—are explained with precision by various writers: Marx 1990; Fishman 2006; Reich 2008; Shell 2010).

So the effects of market capitalism appear in the novel: the tramp is left homeless after he is laid off because his business replaced him with a machine. The presence of the tramp's experience in the novel proves that Sheldon had some idea of the negative consequences of capitalism. However, while the novel criticizes profiteering as selfish, never is the capitalist system subjected to substantial criticism. In fact, the one character in the novel who criticizes "the whole of our system" is immediately dismissed by the other characters (see Boyer 1971, 65). The actual *cause* of the tramp's suffering is noted but set aside, and the novel goes on to chastise Christians for not helping people in the tramp's position. This is, of course, the classic problem of recommending a Band-Aid to cover up a symptom rather than getting at the heart of the problem. The sorts of exploitation of children Marx documented and criticized were not corrected until systematic labor laws were put in place to protect children from those kinds of exploitation. Rather than propose substantial changes to the system, Sheldon redirects attention away from the root disease and instead proposes placing a Band-Aid where symptoms appear. In addition, Sheldon replaces a possible critique of the causes of poverty at the time with a critique of the "Satan of rum." As one commentator puts it:

> The pejoratives that Sheldon attached to the slum dwellers pack a powerful, inadvertent message. Why fight for social and

> economic justice, for a living wage or an eight-hour day or unemployment insurance? These people are incorrigible. Their sins drive them into poverty. And, despite all the big-hearted missionary efforts, they refuse to repent, reform, and rise. (Morone 2003, 245)

Since they are responsible for their own poverty—rather than a capitalist system that replaces people with machines—why bother doing anything systematic to help? The novel leaves the reader with the impression that it may not be worth the bother.

Why this act of misdirection? Why might Sheldon focus on license and saloons rather than the stated causes of the tramp's misfortune? We cannot, of course, know what might have motivated Sheldon. Perhaps it was ignorance, or perhaps he simply believed that alcohol is literally demonic. Either way, we can see that this act of misdirection is one that could, in some instances, serve the interests of his class. The way that the hierarchy between laborers and Maxwell's "professional" class was set up tended to make it easier for members of the professional class to serve their own interests. First, members of wealthier or professional classes profited from the replacement of laborers, insofar as they owned stock for which the value increased as laborers were displaced. Second, the members of the professional class were not subject to the same sort of displacement. Third, members of the professional class simply experienced a great deal of social privileges that resulted from class distinction and the coordinated collusion; were class distinctions obliterated they would lose those privileges (such as the privilege—seen in the novel—to hire people who shared their own habitus). The interests of the professional class Sheldon apparently identifies with would be better served were the system of collusion and domination to remain in place; the maintenance of the status quo was better for the professional class than the working class. For Sheldon to challenge the system that produces these privileges for the professional class would be for him to risk working against his own class's interests. We cannot know why Sheldon drew attention away from the cause of the tramp's poverty, but we can know that avoiding those systemic causes could have reinforced the class domination from which Sheldon's class benefitted.

Analysis: Authority and Projection

The members of the pact in Sheldon's novel are absolutely certain that Jesus would use his abilities to oppose "license" and "saloonism." We can, however, ask the question: is it possible that they are projecting their values onto the figure of Jesus?

What do we know about Jesus and alcohol? There is not much information to be had in the Bible. It appears that just about everyone in the Christian scriptures drinks alcohol (with a few exceptions, like Samson or John the Baptist). In a few places the Christian scriptures prohibit drunkenness. However, Jesus never appears to have prohibited the use of alcohol. In fact, there are stories where he is said to drink alcohol (including the "Last Supper"), and in the gospel of Luke he admits to drinking, and that he has even been accused of being a drunkard (although here he is referring to himself in the third person as the "Son of Man"): "For John the Baptist has come eating no bread and drinking no wine, and you say 'He has a demon'; the Son of Man has come eating and drinking, and you say, 'Look, a glutton and a drunkard, a friend of tax collectors and sinners!'" (Luke 7:33–4). It is unclear whether he sees the accusation of "drunkard" as fair (he doubtlessly assumes that the parallel charge that John is demonic is false), but either way he claims to be a drinker. Apart from this there is little of note about Jesus and alcohol, apart from a rather significant story in the gospel of John. According to John, Jesus' first miracle was to turn water into wine at a wedding. Here is the story:

> On the third day there was a wedding in Cana of Galilee, and the mother of Jesus was there. Jesus and his disciples had also been invited to the wedding. When the wine gave out, the mother of Jesus said to him, "They have no wine." And Jesus said to her, "Woman, what concern is that to you and to me? My hour has not yet come." His mother said to the servants, "Do whatever he tells you." Now standing there were six stone water-jars for the Jewish rites of purification, each holding twenty or thirty gallons. Jesus said to them, "Fill the jars with water." And they filled them up to the brim. He said to them, "Now draw some out, and take it to the chief steward." So they took it. When the steward tasted the water that had become

> wine, and did not know where it came from (though the servants who had drawn the water knew), the steward called the bridegroom and said to him, "Everyone serves the good wine first, and then the inferior wine after the guests have become drunk. But you have kept the good wine until now." Jesus did this, the first of his signs, in Cana of Galilee, and revealed his glory; and his disciples believed in him. (John 2:1–11)

What is particularly telling is that this event is remarkable to the steward *not* because it is miraculous (the steward is not aware that this was a miracle), but because the wedding party seems to have saved the best wine for last. This is remarkable because what normally happens is that expensive wine is produced until people are drunk, at which point the cheap stuff is brought out—since at this point the guests can no longer tell the difference. What this implies is that Jesus has converted water into wine *after* everyone is drunk—otherwise the steward's amazement does not make any sense.

Of course, we do not know if this story ever took place; and, in fact, if we're assuming a hermeneutic of suspicion, we need to be sceptical as a matter of course. Perhaps this story never happened and was instead invented by the author of this gospel. However, Sheldon's form of Christianity probably saw these biblical miracles as literally having taken place. If that is the case, this leaves us with a key question: when Sheldon insists (through the voice of Maxwell) that Jesus would definitely have been opposed to license, is he *projecting* his values onto his favorite authoritative figure (based on what he could know about this figure given his knowledge of the Bible)? The charge that projection is taking place is not only possible, but plausible. It is also worth noting that, insofar as Sheldon's version of Jesus is tied up with capitalist class distinctions that simply did not exist in the first century when Jesus lived, those elements of Sheldon's Jesus are beyond doubt projected.

It is clear why Sheldon might have used the figure of Jesus: Jesus carried a broad authority in Sheldon's social context, an authority that Sheldon by himself could not possibly have held. If Sheldon could successfully project his values onto Jesus, he might more easily legitimate his favored social agenda.

Conclusion

If we apply a hermeneutic of suspicion to Sheldon's novel, focusing on the questions "who is speaking?," "to whom?," "in what context?," and "if persuasive, who stands to gain and who stands to lose?," we get a very interesting set of answers. Sheldon is speaking primarily to a professional Christian audience, in late nineteenth-century America. The context of the novel and its reception is a nation sharply divided into the working class and wealthier classes. If Sheldon was persuasive—and there is evidence he was: the book was an instant bestseller (Boyer 1971, 61)—what might the effects have been? Obviously, one social agenda Sheldon hoped to advance was the prohibition of the sale of alcohol. And, in fact, Sheldon was one of many Christian propagandists writing and working in the late nineteenth century and early twentieth century whose propaganda was, in fact, persuasive; their efforts resulted in precisely what they desired: prohibition. That is, works like Sheldon's were so broadly persuasive that the United States passed an amendment to their constitution (about twenty years after Sheldon's novel appeared) forbidding the sale of alcohol. Obviously, Sheldon and *In His Steps* were not solely responsible for prohibition, but his work was one of many in support of the agenda that eventually won.

Who stood to gain and who stood to lose? Obviously, those people who sold and consumed alcohol stood to lose. In addition, as I have demonstrated, working class people stood to lose from Sheldon's novel—to the extent that it was persuasive—insofar as it taught wealthy people that the working class was not only different because of dress and habit (i.e., habitus), but perhaps also demonic. Despite Sheldon's apparent hope that class lines would be crossed (that is, he seemed to want Christians to convert working class people to Christianity), his implicit demonization of the working class as a whole would probably have had the effect of sharpening class divisions. Given the way that class habitus works, and given the way that the differences in habitus were reinforced in the novel as divine on the one side and demonic on the other, those members of Maxwell's class would be less likely to extend privileges to those outside their class and more likely to discriminate. To the extent that it was persuasive in the context in which it originally appeared, this novel worked to reflect and reinforce the domination of wealthy classes over and against the working class.

This chapter, then, shows how one could apply the methods and theory of religion proposed in this book to Sheldon's novel, and that doing so sheds light on "what's going on" with Sheldon's form of late nineteenth-century Christianity. Sheldon's *In His Steps* is a great artifact for demonstrating the usefulness of critical terms such as habitus, domination, legitimation, authority, and projection.

Afterword

This book has not offered a comprehensive explanation of religion or how religious traditions work. Instead, it is an introduction to how religious traditions can be used to create, maintain, and contest social order. My purpose has been to introduce readers to what I find to be the most useful concepts for thinking critically about religions:

- a hermeneutic of suspicion,
- functionalism,
- classification,
- social constructions and social constructionism,
- group boundaries,
- social hierarchy and social positions,
- assigned behaviors such as social roles, moral norms, and behavioral codes,
- socialization,
- habitus,
- normalization,
- discrimination,
- privilege,
- reproduction/maintenance of social order or the status quo,
- contestation of the status quo,
- reification/naturalization/mystification,
- desire and repression,
- interests and domination,
- legitimation,

- cultural toolbox and cultural tools,
- authority and projection, and
- authenticity claims.

These concepts permit us to answer these sorts of critical questions:

- In general, *how are religious traditions used to create, shape, or modify societies or social groups*?
- How do cultural tools function to reflect and reinforce:
  - group boundaries?
  - social hierarchies?
  - social roles, moral norms, etc.?
- For any given religious text or interpretation of a religious text, who is trying to convince whom of what? What would be the social implications or social consequences if the text or interpretation were received as persuasive?
- How does a shared habitus sustain social classes, social relations, social boundaries, "normal" practices, etc.? How can a shared habitus be connected to one's religious tradition?

My interest in these issues is the same as Bruce Lincoln's when he claims the following:

> even the most pacific and seemingly benevolent of these rituals still serve to produce subjects who will thereafter accept the propositions, statuses, and modes of being that society desires for and demands of them: persons whom it can use for its own purposes, as productive workers, for example, docile spouses, nurturant mothers, or anaesthetized lovers (in the last case, I think particularly of the many initiatory rituals that feature clitoridectomy). In truth, persuasion can be more insidious than coercion, for while the latter generally provokes some measure of resentment and resistance, skillful persuasion can avoid sowing these seeds of future struggle, insofar as it leads its subjects to desire … for themselves precisely what society desires of them. (Lincoln 1991, 112)

Here Lincoln is talking about rituals that reinforce the subordination of women, but what he is describing could extend to all elements of cultural toolboxes. If we are attentive to how domination is reinforced, we can more easily resist its pull.

In Mark Twain's *Huckleberry Finn*, which is set in the United States prior to its Civil War, a young boy named Huck Finn runs away from his foster mother's home along with a slave named Jim. Because of his nineteenth-century, conservative Christian upbringing, Huck experiences a great deal of guilt because he feels that by helping Jim escape he has basically stolen Jim from his foster mother, and as such he has committed a sin that will doom him to hell. Helping Jim escape was a "low-down thing" (Twain 1885, 270). Huck thinks to himself,

> The more I studied about this, the more my conscience went to grinding me, and the more wicked and low-down and ornery I got to feeling. And at last, when it hit me all of the sudden that here was the plain hand of Providence [i.e., God] slapping me in the face and letting me know my wickedness was being watched all the time from up there in heaven, whilst I was stealing a poor old woman's nigger that hadn't ever done me no harm, and now was showing me there's One [i.e., God] that's always on the lookout, and ain't agoing to allow no such miserable things to go only just fur and no further, I most dropped in my tracks I was so scared. (Twain 1885, 270)

He admits that people who steal go "to everlasting fire" (Twain 1885, 270), and he decides to repent and make right what he has done. So he sits down and writes out a letter to his foster mother, telling her what happened and where she can find Jim. However, although he felt "clean of sin" upon having written the letter, he soon begins reflecting on Jim's interests, rather than his own. He thinks about what Jim had done for him, and about the fact that he was Jim's only friend left in the world. In the middle of these thoughts,

> I happened to look around, and see that paper.
>
> It was a close place. I took it up, and held it in my hand. I was a trembling, because I'd got to decide, forever, between two things, and I knowed it. I studied for a minute, sort of holding my breath, and then says to myself:
>
> "All right, then, I'll *go* to hell"—and tore it up.
>
> (Twain 1885, 271–2; emphasis original)

Like Huck Finn, we are all surrounded by social orders that serve the interests of some at the expense of others, and we have been subjected to legitimations that make those exploitative power relations seem natural, right, and fair—and we have often been told that to violate the social codes we've inherited will result in cosmic consequences. However, like Huck Finn, some of us have the ability to compare what seems natural or divine with how human interests are served by the social orders that are regularly legitimated by appeals to nature and divinity.

If we pay more attention to all the things that are naturalized for us or that we take for granted, it will be easier for us to identify and reconsider disproportionate social structures. Like Huck Finn, some of us may choose to "go to hell" if "going to heaven" means participating in the reproduction of exploitative social relations.

References

Abbott, Lyman. 1899. *Christianity and Social Problems*. Boston, MA: Houghton, Mifflin and Company.

Althusser, Louis. 2001. *Lenin and Philosophy and Other Essays*. Ben Brewster, trans. New York: Monthly Review Press.

Althusser, Louis. 2008. *On Ideology*. London: Verso.

Arnal, William. 2005. *The Symbolic Jesus: Historical Scholarship, Judaism and the Construction of Contemporary Identity*. London: Equinox Publishing.

Avalos, Hector. 2007. *The End of Biblical Studies*. Amherst, NY: Prometheus Books.

Avalos, Hector. 2009. "Is Biblical Illiteracy a Bad Thing? Reflections on Bibliolatry in the Modern Academy." *Council of Societies for the Study of Religion Bulletin* 38/2: 47–52.

Baggini, Julian. 2006. *The Pig that Wants to Be Eaten: 100 Experiments for the Armchair Philosopher*. New York: Plume.

Baxter, Richard. 2000. *The Practical Works of Richard Baxter, Vol. I: A Christian Directory*. Morgan, PA: Soli Deo Gloria Publications.

Bayart, Jean-François. 2005. *The Illusion of Cultural Identity*. Steven Rendall, Janet Rottman, Cynthia Schoch, and Jonathan Derrick, trans. Chicago, IL: University of Chicago Press.

Berger, Peter. 1967. *The Sacred Canopy: Elements of a Sociological Theory of Religion*. New York: Doubleday.

Berger, Peter and Thomas Luckmann. 1967. *The Social Construction of Reality: A Treatise in the Sociology of Knowledge*. New York: Doubleday.

Botham, Fay. 2009. *Almighty God Created the Races: Christianity, Interracial Marriage, and American Law*. Chapel Hill, NC: University of North Carolina Press.

Bottici, Chiara. 2007. *A Philosophy of Political Myth*. Cambridge, UK: Cambridge University Press.

Bourdieu, Pierre. 1984. *Distinction: A Social Critique of the Judgment of Taste*. Richard Nice, trans. Cambridge, MA: Harvard University Press.

Bourdieu, Pierre. 1990. *The Logic of Practice*. Stanford, CA: Stanford University Press.

Bourdieu, Pierre. 1998. *Practical Reason: On the Theory of Action*. Stanford, CA: Stanford University Press.

Bourdieu, Pierre. 1999. *Language and Symbolic Power*. Cambridge, MA: Harvard University Press.

Boyer, Paul S. 1971. "*In His Steps*: A Reappraisal." *American Quarterly* 23/1: 60–78.

Boyer, Paschal. 2002. *Religion Explained: The Evolutionary Origins of Religious Thought*. New York: Basic Books.

Butler, Judith. 1990. *Gender Trouble: Feminism and the Subversion of Identity*. London: Routledge.

Cohen, Anthony P. 1985. *The Symbolic Construction of Community*. London: Routledge.

Cook, Michael. 2000. *The Koran: A Very Short Introduction*. Oxford, UK: Oxford University Press.

Douglas, Mary. 1986. *How Institutions Think*. Syracuse, NY: Syracuse University Press.

Durkheim, Émile. 1982. *The Rules of Sociological Method*. W. D. Halls, trans. New York: Free Press.

Durkheim, Émile. 2001. *The Elementary Forms of Religious Life*. Carol Cosman, trans. Oxford, UK: Oxford University Press.

Ehrman, Bart D. 1999a. *Jesus: Apocalyptic Prophet of the New Millennium*. Oxford, UK: Oxford University Press.

Ehrman, Bart D. 1999b. *After the New Testament: A Reader in Early Christianity*. Oxford, UK: Oxford University Press.

Epley, Nicholas, Benjamin A. Converse, Alexa Delbosc, George A. Monteleone and John T. Cacioppo. 2009. "Believers' Estimates of God's Beliefs are More Egocentric than Estimates of Other People's Beliefs." *Proceedings of the National Academy of Sciences of the United States of America* 105/51: 21,533–8.

Fausto-Sterling, Anne. 1993. "The Five Sexes." *The Sciences* March/April: 20–5.

Fausto-Sterling, Anne. 2000. *Sexing the Body: Gender Politics and the Construction of Sexuality*. New York: Basic Books.

Fishman, Charles. 2006. *The Wal-Mart Effect: How the World's Most Powerful Company Really Works—And How It's Transforming the American Economy*. New York: Penguin.

Freud, Sigmund. 1989. *The Future of an Illusion*. James Strachey, ed. New York: W. W. Norton & Company.

Frontline. 1985. "A Class Divided." A program in the *Frontline* television series, originally broadcast in 1985. The description quoted here is from the PBS channel's website (undated), available at www.pbs.org/wgbh/pages/frontline/shows/divided/etc/credits.html.

Gandhi, Mohandas Karamchand. 2000. *The Bhagavad Gita according to Gandhi*. Berkeley, CA: Berkeley Hills Books.

Giddens, Anthony. 1984. *The Constitution of Society*. Berkeley, CA: University of California Press.

Gluckman, Max. 1965. *Politics, Law, and Ritual in Tribal Society*. Chicago, IL: Aldine.

Goodall, Dominic, ed. 1996. *Hindu Scriptures*. Berkeley, CA: University of California Press.

Grant, Robert M. 1997. *Irenaeus of Lyons*. London: Routledge.

Hacking, Ian. 2002. *Historical Ontology*. Cambridge, MA: Harvard University Press.

Hagerty, Barbara Bradley. 2010. "Is the Bible More Violent than the Quran?" *National Public Radio*, 21 March. Available at www.npr.org/templates/story/story.php?storyId=124494788&ps=cprs.

Haleem, M. A. S. Abdel, trans. 2004. *The Qur'an*. Oxford, UK: Oxford University Press.

Hammer, Olav, ed. 2009. *Alternative Christs*. Cambridge, UK: Cambridge University Press.

Hammer, Olav and James R. Lewis, eds. 2007. *The Invention of Sacred Tradition*. Cambridge, UK: Cambridge University Press.

Hooker, Richard. 1989. *Of the Laws of Ecclesiastical Policy*. Arthur Stephen McGrade, ed. Cambridge, UK: Cambridge University Press.

Hughes, Aaron W. 2007. *Situating Islam: The Past and Future of an Academic Discipline*. London: Equinox.

Ingersoll, Julie. 2003. *Evangelical Christian Women: War Stories in the Gender Battles*. New York: New York University Press.

Jha, J. N. 2009. *Rethinking Hindu Identity*. London: Equinox Publishing.

Kertzer, David. 1988. *Ritual, Politics, and Power*. New Haven, CT: Yale University Press.

Lincoln, Bruce. 1981. *Emerging from the Chrysalis: Studies in Rituals of Women's Initiation*. Cambridge, MA: Harvard University Press.

Lincoln, Bruce. 1989. *Discourse and the Construction of Society: Comparative Studies of Myth, Ritual, and Classification*. Chicago, IL: Chicago University Press.

Lincoln, Bruce. 1991a. *Death, War, and Sacrifice: Studies in Ideology and Practice*. Chicago, IL: University of Chicago Press.

Lincoln, Bruce. 1991b. *Emerging from the Chrysalis: Studies in Rituals of Women's Initiation*. Chicago, IL: University of Chicago Press.

Lincoln, Bruce. 1994. *Authority: Construction and Corrosion*. Chicago, IL: University of Chicago Press.

Lincoln, Bruce. 1996. "Theses on Method." *Method and Theory in the Study of Religion* 8: 225–7.

Lincoln, Bruce. 2006. "How to Read a Religious Text." *History of Religions* 46/2: 127–39.

Lincoln, Bruce. 2007. *Religion, Empire, and Torture: The Case of Achaemenian Persia, with a Postscript on Abu Ghraib*. Chicago, IL: University of Chicago Press.

Lorber, Judith. 1994. *Paradoxes of Gender*. New Haven, CT: Yale University Press.

Lui, Meizhu, ed. 2006. *The Color of Wealth: The Story behind the U.S. Racial Wealth Divide*. New York: New Press.

Marx, Karl. 1990. *Capital, Volume 1*. Trans. by Ben Fowkes. New York: Penguin.

Marx, Karl and Friedrich Engels. 1998. *The Communist Manifesto*. London: Verso.

McCutcheon, Russell. 2001. *Critics not Caretakers: Redescribing the Public Study of Religion*. Albany, NY: State University of New York Press.

McCutcheon, Russell. 2005. *Religion and the Domestication of Dissent: Or, How to Live in a Less than Perfect Nation*. London: Equinox.

Miller, Barbara Stoler, trans. 1986. *The Bhagavad Gita: Krishna's Council in Time of War*. New York: Bantam.

Misra, R. L. 2004. *Identity and Religion: Foundations of Anti-Islamism in India*. New Delhi, India: Sage Publications.

Mohanty, Satya P. 1997. *Literary Theory and the Claims of History: Postmodernism, Objectivity, Multicultural Politics*. Ithaca, NY: Cornell University Press.

Morone, James A. 2003. *Hellfire Nation: The Politics of Sin in American History*. New Haven, CT: Yale University Press.

Murphy, Tim. 2007. *Representing Religion: Essays in History, Theory, and Crisis*. London: Equinox Publishing.

Nanda, Serena. 2000. *Gender Diversity: Crosscultural Variations*. Long Grove, IL: Waveland Press.

Needham, Rodney. 1979. *Symbolic Classification*. Santa Monica, CA: Goodyear Publishing Company.

Nye, Malory. 2008. *Religion: The Basics, Second Edition*. London: Routledge.

Pagels, Elaine. 1979. *The Gnostic Gospels*. New York: Random House.

Pape, Robert A. 2005. *Dying to Win: The Strategic Logic of Suicide Terrorism*. New York: Random House.

Pelikan, Jaroslav. 1985. *Jesus through the Centuries: His Place in the History of Culture*. New Haven, CT: Yale University Press.

Prothero, Stephen. 2003. *American Jesus: How the Son of God became a National Icon*. New York: Farrar, Straus, and Giroux.

Putnam, Hilary. 2004. *Ethics without Ontology*. Cambridge, MA: Harvard University Press.

Reich, Robert. 2008. *Supercapitalism: The Transformation of Business, Democracy, and Everyday Life*. New York: Random House.

Rogerson, J. W. 2007. *According to the Scriptures? The Challenge of Using the Bible in Social, Moral, and Political Questions*. London: Equinox Publishing.

Rothstein, Mikael. 2007. "Scientology, Scripture, and Tradition," in *The Invention of Sacred Tradition*. James R. Lewis and Olav Hammer, ed. Cambridge, UK: Cambridge University Press.

Rousseau, Jean-Jacques. 1983. *The Essential Rousseau*. Lowell Bair, trans. New York: Meridian.

Sahlins, Marshall. 1987. *Islands of History*. Chicago, IL: University of Chicago Press.

Schiappa, Edward. 2003. *Defining Reality: Definitions and the Politics of Meaning*. Carbondale, IL: Southern Illinois University Press.

Schweitzer, Albert. 1910. *The Quest of the Historical Jesus*. London: A. & C. Black.

Sheldon, Charles M. 1899. *In His Steps*. Chicago, IL: Advance Publishing Co.

Shell, Ellen Ruppel. 2010. *Cheap: The High Cost of Discount Culture*. New York: Penguin.

Smith, Brian K. 1989. *Reflections on Resemblance, Ritual, and Religion*. New York: Oxford University Press.

Smith, Jonathan Z. 2004. *Relating Religion: Essays in the Study of Religion*. Chicago, IL: University of Chicago Press.
Swartz, David. 1997. *Culture and Power: The Sociology of Pierre Bourdieu*. Chicago, IL: University of Chicago Press.
Twain, Mark. 1885. *Adventures of Huckleberry Finn (Tom Sawyer's Comrade)*. New York: Charles L. Webster and Company. Facsimile of first edition available at http://openlibrary.org/books/OL7244099M/Adventures_of_Huckleberry_Finn
Watson, Burton, trans. 2002. *The Essential Lotus: Selections from the Lotus Sutra*. New York: Columbia University Press.
Welch, Gina. 2010. *In the Land of Believers: An Outsider's Extraordinary Journey into the Heart of the Evangelical Church*. New York: Metropolitan Books.
Williams, Raymond. 1977. *Marxism and Literature*. Oxford, UK: Oxford University Press.
Williams, Raymond. 1981. *The Sociology of Culture*. New York: Schocken Books.

Index